# MACKENZIE
# ON
# MANAGING
# COMMUNICATIONS

# MACKENZIE
# ON
# MANAGING
# COMMUNICATIONS

## Jude Mackenzie

Indie*B*ooks

Mackenzie on Managing Communications
By Jude Mackenzie
Studies in Strategic Communications II

© Jude Mackenzie 2019

Published by IndieBooks Limited, London

ISBN: 978-1-908041-074

Printed by Printondemand-worldwide, Peterborough

*To my parents, Pam and John,
and my husband, Alistair*

# Contents

# Preface

*"Half the money I spend on advertising is wasted;
the trouble is, I don't know which half."*

This quotation has been ascribed to a variety of business leaders, but whoever coined it, one thing is certain: it captures a truth not only about communications, but about the difficulty of managing communications.

Imagine an industry in which half the machines you install to make your product don't work; or where half the people you employ to deliver a service stand idly by. Imagine the frustration this situation creates for the managing director, the board and the shareholders – knowing there is a vast wastage of capital and labour, but not knowing where it lies – and their response when a manager cheerfully reassures them that at least half is working.

This frustration will be familiar to anyone who has been on the board of an organisation, or been responsible to the senior leadership for communications in all its different forms, from digital marketing to employee engagement. We may know that these different forms of communication 'work': but we often struggle to prove it, or demonstrate that doing things differently would produce a different outcome. And this in turn produces a new challenge – how to manage commuications in a way that is honest about these difficulties, and yet still gives some reassurance and sense of control to those more used to dealing in the reassurance of 'hard' financial numbers or the precision of systems engineering.

This is the challenge that this book sets out to meet.

And no-one is better placed to write it than Jude Mackenzie, whose career has covered every aspect of communications, and taken her from the magazine staffer to the board of one of Britain's most respected charities, and includes rebranding the NHS along the way. Her audience includes heads of communicaton, and communications professionals whose careers are now taking them into board-level discussions. But it also extends to those board members, who may for the first time be faced with the particular challenges of getting the best from communications spending, and also building comms into their business planning – particularly in areas such as risk management and resilience.

Jude's approach is to review each of the building-blocks of communications, drawing out the key points of how these can support an organisation in achieving its goals. Then she looks at how these blocks come together in planning and preparation. And as seems only right in a discipline which draws heavily on psychology, sociology and plain human nature, she offers wise advice on the human factor, both engaging with others and developing the self-knowledge that can make a career in communications rewarding in so many ways.

James Humphreys
*Series Editor*

# Introduction

## Why is this important?

Which are the most successful organisations? The ones that make the most money, have the most impact, work most efficiently? And which ones do that? It's the ones that have the most support from people – customers, staff, stakeholders, the general public. You could have the most noble purpose in the world or make the best products but if people don't like you – or key groups particularly don't like you, you are toast.

And the converse is true. You may have the most awful purpose or make awful products – but if key groups like you, you can fly.

Every board and senior team needs to think about reputation and stakeholder management. These are the disciplines usually covered by the term 'communications' or 'comms' for short. This book is about how comms is understood and delivered by the top team of an organisation, especially the director of comms.

When BBC radio first started, the Prime Minister of the day was asked whether there was anything he would like to say to the nation. Not the toughest interview question ever.

This was the fact that my former boss Alastair Campbell often quoted in his speeches on how comms has changed. We now live in a 24-hour news world of tough, aggressive questioning where citizen journalists and online commentators outnumber traditional media outlets. At the same time, society has changed: the so-called death of deference means that people don't have the respect for government, public institutions and traditionally-trusted brands that they used to.  There is less slack for getting things wrong, and a higher expectation of transparency.

These changes mean the job of comms has changed vastly. And the job of managing comms has and will change constantly. This is a book about the latter. There are lots of books on the practicalities of public relations, public affairs, digital comms, market research and corporate communications.   I couldn't find a book on conducting the comms orchestra – stepping up and managing a comms team and representing comms on the senior management team.

This book is my observations, from a thirty-year career in comms, on managing comms at board level.  My target audience for this book is comms directors (or aspiring comms directors), and chief executives and other directors that need to understand the issues.

As a chief executive, or other director, you will have become very accomplished in your chosen field.  Perhaps you are adept at product design, understanding international policy, delivering huge infrastructure projects or dealing with million-pound budgets.

And then you are on a board that also needs to think about a social media campaign that is targeting your record on use of renewable energy, or a general public that stubbornly refuse to ignore scientific evidence about their own behaviour.

You want change to happen. You want to help your board achieve the objectives of the business, but you know that you need to deal with those pesky people issues in order to do it. What's your frame of reference?

Or you may be the director of comms. You may have become very accomplished at doing the day job: the perfectly-crafted tweet, the best damage-limitation news release,  the barnstorming event.  You then take on a director role and find you need a new set of skills that you may not have acquired on the way unless you had a forward-thinking boss who let you deputise.  Suddenly the intricacies of making something happen in a larger organisation become your daily worry. You have to think about the whole picture, not just your little part of it.

Or perhaps you are the director in charge of comms, but it isn't your own skill set.  What are the questions you should be asking your team?

As directors you share corporate responsibility for the whole organisation's success and failure.  All of you need to decide together what to fund, what to support, what initiatives to close down – even if they are initiatives in your own department.  This is a hard one to defend when you get back to your own team, but it is part of corporate governance. You need some understanding of the different disciplines around the senior management table.

This book explains how to understand the comms issues, and why they are important. As I am straddling different levels of expertise in comms, some of the content might seem a bit obvious for an experienced comms person. But I hope that are also sufficient insights from living the reality of being director of comms to provoke some thinking for experienced readers.

I have worked in some of the toughest comms environments.  In Government, including at 10 Downing Street, in the National Health Service, in social care, in the property business and in charities. These sectors have a plethora of audiences that they need to listen and respond to, and they aren't always friendly. They don't always have a clear 'bottom line' – you need to define success and failure together with your colleagues and stakeholders.  Having said that, the principles shared in this book will work across all sectors – profit and non-profit. Strategic planning, influencing upwards and outwards and managing your team are roles that will be common to every comms director.

I need to give credit here to the chairs, chief executives and directors that I have worked with for much of the wisdom that I repeat in this book. And, I need to extend an apology to the people who have worked for me who might wish, on reading this, that I had learnt some of these lessons sooner. Thank you for your patience.

## What do we mean by communications?

Communications ('comms') incorporates many professional disciplines. This book focuses on the main ones listed below.

***Media and social media.*** You have been campaigning for people to respect wildlife for years and years with only small success. The peak-time BBC show Blue Planet graphically shows birds and fish dying from plastic pollution. Nine in ten people that watch the show report changing how they use plastic. Social media is awash with anti-plastic messaging. Starbucks and McDonalds announce that they are phasing out plastic straws. How your organisation and your issues are represented in the media has a huge impact on your success.

***Internal comms.*** You employ 4,000 staff in 20 different locations. The staff survey comes back every year saying that people trust their own team but not the senior management. They say they don't understand the vision of the organisation and they are worried about their future. Internal comms underlines that your staff are your most valuable asset, and your most valuable ambassadors. How do you ensure that they are positively engaged?

**Strategy and planning.** Your comms department is incredibly busy. There isn't a spare moment in the day when they aren't firefighting, responding to a Twitter storm and planning for your set-piece big event. But can you be sure that all this activity is adding up to progress towards your main goals? How can you get your comms strategy and planning right so that you increase activity that has impact, and limit activity that doesn't?

**Stakeholder management.** You are a busy chief executive, but you seem to spend endless hours discussing how to respond to a small pressure group that have launched a vitriolic campaign against what you are doing. At the same time, the regulator that covers your issues is due to make a huge decision about your future, and you find you haven't spoken to their senior team for months. How you and your organisation prioritise and manage your relationships with stakeholders will be the difference between success and failure in many cases.

**Brand management.** Your organisation has made huge technological advances and now leads the sector in innovative models. Yet your logo and personality still sit in last century and stakeholders think of you as safe but boring. How can you update what you look like as an organisation without losing your core values? Branding is the way that you show yourself to the world and affects what the public will think about you.

**Public affairs.** Public opinion is driving political decisions that will have a huge impact on your work. New legislation that is being drafted is populist and could open up massive unforeseen pitfalls. Public affairs is how you engage with government and other political stakeholders to maximise the chances of achieving your goals.

**Campaigns.** All the credible research points to the need for change. However, the public and government just don't want to change. You need to launch a high-profile, long-running campaign to persuade people that change is vital.

**Research and evaluation.** You are sitting around the board room table and one of the non-executives tells you that their friend's son works in a sector allied to yours and he and all his colleagues think that you should launch a new initiative. How do you ensure that your comms plans are based on proper research of what people think, and not driven by just personal experience or one person's view?

**Crisis management.** It's 11pm at night and you get the awful phone call that tells you that a fire has ruined one of your big warehouses and three people are missing. You immediately launch the crisis management protocol and, among the many tasks that are pressing, the decision on how to make your own announcement about the news and reassure the public and your own staff is a priority.

These different disciplines are explored in part one of this book. Part two then looks at the specifics on how to operate as a comms director and run a comms department. These may not be all that is in the comms director's remit. Marketing, customer or user engagement, fundraising, customer services, complaints, policy and digital are often your responsibility, too. However, I think the disciplines that I have covered in this book are usually at the core of the role.

# Part One: Communications at the Top Table

## Chapter One

# Media, Social Media and Content Creation

- **Why is media so important?**
- **How do you 'go viral' in a positive way?**
- **Can you control your image on social media?**

**Mainstream Media**

The radio alarm blares into life with the headlines of the day. Still half asleep I hear the sentence, "Health campaigners have expressed outrage at the latest revelations from a hospital in…" and pray silently "please, not my region." If the sentence finishes "Manchester" it may be a difficult time for my colleagues in the north, but I can get up and get my tea in peace. The dreaded sentence changed subject as I moved from job to job, but the feeling never went. Would my day be ruined?

Or scenario two: it's Sunday and I jump out of bed and rush to the newsagents to buy the Sunday Times. Tea in hand I flick quickly through the magazine because the journalist I have been working with for the last two months tells me the article will be in today. My heart soars when the page falls open - a great picture and a good headline. My organisation isn't mentioned until paragraph 14, but it's a good day.

Media coverage – it can make or break your day. And that's true whether you are the communications director, the chief executive or the person meeting customers at the front line.

In my experience, comms directors fall into two camps. There are those for whom a breaking story is the highlight of the day, a wave of energy that they will happily surf on for days, delighted that it means they have a good excuse not to do the other stuff in their inbox. Or there are those who see it as a crashing tidal wave that ruins their week, stopping them from getting on with all the other things they had planned.

Love it or hate it, media relations is nearly always the core of the comms director's job which is why it's the first chapter. It's often 80 per cent of what chief execs think the comms director is there for and 80 per cent of what they are interested in.     And, depending on the comms director's background, it might be 80 per cent of what they think the job is about, too.    It isn't necessarily the most important channel that we use, but it is powerful and potentially dangerous. The comms director's role is sometimes like a lion tamer – ensuring that her employers don't get eaten for breakfast by a hungry media pack.

I switched from journalism to PR fairly early in my career but I can still remember the mild feeling of superiority that I had as a journalist, the advantage that I thought I had understanding how journalists think, and then the uphill struggle, but also delight, when I realised that I had so much else to learn.

What makes the media even more powerful is the symbiotic relationship between the traditional media and social media. Politicians and campaigners use social media to break stories and so news media outlets are increasingly taking their cues from Twitter. US president Donald Trump is the best example. Love it or hate it, the media cannot be ignored.

As director you will need to ensure that you have good people on your media desk because of the power of the bad, or good, headline. Arguably it's the most important job in your team to get right.

Here are my top tips. I have split this into 'proactive', 'reactive' and 'general' because there are differences in approach. As you know, proactive coverage is the coverage that your team works to generate. Reactive coverage is when the journalists come to you, quite often with a story that you don't want. For this section, I have focused the reactive tips on coverage that you don't want.

Working in health, there was never a day when we weren't in the media. Working in charity, there were far too many days when we weren't in the media. They require slightly different skills.

**Proactive**
Positive media coverage is like gold-dust, and very valuable to your cause because it comes from an independent voice, and the reach and influence can be huge – in many cases greater than any other comms tactic that you use. So, you need to give your team time, resources and encouragement to generate media coverage.

If you are a chief executive or other director, remember that media messaging is different, so trust your media expert. Here is a scenario that's very familiar to press officers: the date is set for the launch of the new product/new fundraising campaign/ new hard-hitting policy report. You are in the planning meetings and your job is listed as 'get media coverage on 20 May'. The product/fundraising/policy team, rarely media experts, kindly tell you what the messages are that need to be in the media. If they are a bit too forceful in this, you sit round the table, your head metaphorically in your hands, and think – do these people think I just ring up the editor and say 'I'm sending over something for publication; page five would be our preference'?

Most of the disagreements I have had in my comms career have been about media messaging. I think it's the biggest gap in knowledge and understanding that comms people have with non-comms people. The over-excited marketing lines of a new product, the happy joyous messaging for the new fundraising campaign, the niche, beard-stroking conclusions of the new policy report just won't cut it for media.

It isn't easy to get media coverage, and it's even less easy to get it when the only people that care about the subject are essentially your organisation and your gran. So, media lines will often have to be slightly different – the journalists want a story and if that means that the rest of the organisation needs to accept that the 'newer, sleeker, more efficient' message that's being used for everything else can't be used in the press release, so be it.

As a chief executive you might feel nervous because the top line of the press release isn't what you would have written. But that's why you have hired a comms director. If you have a good media team, trust them on this one. As a comms director you will need to stand up for your team's judgment while everyone else on the chain of emails tries to rewrite their top line. There is nothing to be gained at all from having a press release that everyone internally is happy with but doesn't get any coverage whatsoever. That is a waste of time.

Chief executives and directors should also be pleased not offended when the press team develop the questions and answers (Q&A) document containing all the tough questions that the media might ask. 'Why did you give yourself a 30% pay rise? 'You failed in your last two posts, what makes you think this is different?" You have only shut northern offices, are you biased against the North?' You might think the questions are unnecessarily challenging, disloyal and offensive but recognise they are an important part of the preparation for what might come.

Media must fit into a plan – but with space for spontaneity. The media plan should fit into the overall calendar and plan of the comms team so that they know what the big dates are both internally and externally, and what the priority objectives are. The delivery should ensure that, where possible, you are repeating the main messaging that your organisation has agreed (even if subtly.)

However, the plan must also allow for media relations to be spontaneous and take advantage of themes or events that emerge and are part of media and public debate. This is particularly necessary for organisations that seek to be thought leaders. You will want to have something interesting to say and contribute to a live topic, and you must then be willing to prioritise time for your spokespeople to do their preparation and interviews – dropping other things if necessary.

**Reactive**

The email from a Sunday newspaper lands with the press team late on Friday afternoon. 'We have discovered that the manager of your Solihull branch has convictions for drug use and is dealing drugs using your office as a base.' Or, 'we are carrying out a survey of charities funded by oil companies and we believe that you are one. Please send us a list of your major donors by 5pm'.

Or you get a text on your way in to work one morning. *The Mail Online* is running a story that says that our kitchens are the worst the inspector has ever seen. Headline is "Top chef's kitchens branded 'roach motels'".

It sounds obvious to say this, but the senior management team do need to take bad headlines seriously. A bad story, true or not, can catch like wildfire – spreading its negative effects across media and social media within hours. The old adage 'it's tomorrow's chip paper' doesn't apply any more. The paper version might be, the online stuff lives on like that stubborn cockroach.

For this reason, chief executives and directors need to know that there are times when you need to drop everything to deal with a story. Most chief press officers will know that they can talk to the directors' PA to get quick access when required, and this is important.

It's fair to mention that bad stories don't always go wild – there are lots of factors that influence this including what else is happening in the Twittersphere, so judgment is required, but the discussion is necessary, at least.

Plan for surprises. Any chief executive will tell you that the media can blow your plans for the day out of the window, and your career in some extreme cases. It can feel like a ghastly shock, but, as we discuss in the 'crisis management' chapter, most bad stories can be predicted in advance, and planned for or mitigation put in place. Charities, for example, adapted to the new public mood about fundraising methods highlighted in the tragedy of 'Olive Cooke' – the lady who killed herself and had been bombarded with charity requests for money. Even before the legislation changed, wise charities could predict that 'fundraising scandals' were a trending topic with the media and could plan for possible scenarios. Transport companies can plan for accidents, food companies can plan for health scares, and so on.

Sudden or not, bad media stories will eat up time and the rest of the comms team will need to respect that attention has shifted for a while so other things will go on the back burner. Or the rest of the team might get pulled onto managing the bad story – either answering the phones or ensuring that briefings are sent to other stakeholders (including staff).

It's also worth mentioning here that negative stories can be 'killed' if the press team have some warning. But, be aware that killing a story takes time and, if you are lucky, there will be literally nothing to show for it. The press team will need encouragement, protection and acknowledgement if they manage to keep something out of the press.

Sending a briefing note round to the top team about a story that hopefully won't appear is a great way to highlight the hard work that the team has done and reinforce the value of skilled professionals in this role.

There is no such thing as 'off the record'. If you are a chief executive, or board member, be really careful if you are talking to a journalist. It's best to discuss it with your comms director first if you can. Journalists want to bypass the press office and love nothing better than opinion and gossip. So, if they catch you in the bar at an industry event don't think that their generosity in buying you drinks is because they are just a nice person. Don't try to impress them with everything you know about what's happening behind the scenes. I remember a chair I worked with doing that one year and then being surprised when it was all in the Financial Times the next day. When comms directors say everything has to go through the press team there are very good reasons for that so don't just respect it but advocate it to the whole organisation.

Respect the reputational risk radar. Comms directors, and chief press officers especially, usually have the best radar on reputational risk. If you don't have a comms professional on the board or the top team then try to find a way to harness their early-warning system on what could make a bad headline. This is particularly true if you have a non-comms professional representing comms on the board. And if you are the comms director, speak up. I have been frequently surprised by how other senior members of staff understandably don't have the intuition to know that an idea or action might play very badly in the press and therefore risk harming the reputation of the organisation.

**General**
Choose spokespeople wisely. If the press team could place an online order for the perfect spokesperson it would be: speaks clearly and without jargon; talks like a human being; has a nice voice; is willing to drop other things to do a radio interview at short notice; knows their subject.

Here is what they often get: talks as if trying to impress their board colleagues – full of jargon and no humanity; sounds patronising; hardly ever makes themselves available because doesn't really like doing it; wants a Q&A 15 pages long even for a two-minute interview; refuses to have their training updated because they 'did that 10 years ago and it was awful'.   It's understandable. If I was not the comms director, I would probably have been this person!  Tough media interviews aren't anybody's favourite pastime.

However, it's inevitable that if you are on the senior management team you may need to be a spokesperson, if you are chief executive you will need to.  Make sure you get trained properly by someone outside your press team who will be honest with you and give you experience of different settings – radio, TV, live, print etc.

Accept that if your organisation is making a major press statement the radio and TV stations will then call asking for interviews.  Clear your diary and make yourself available (there is no way round this!)

If you are the comms director, you will often take the lead in choosing the spokesperson. Then you might be in the difficult position of having to decide that some spokespeople just aren't good enough.  It's not a personal criticism, it's just not a skill that everyone has.  Perhaps their accent is too strong, their style is too defensive and nervous, or they just go to pieces when there is a microphone in front of them. It's OK, for most occasions, to choose someone better.  A good interviewee is nearly always better than the 'right' person doing a bad job.  If someone hates doing interviews, I don't think it's worth pushing them too much because it just shows.  Perhaps they can be involved in other ways – some one-to-one stakeholder conversations or reviewing written material.

You won't find many people that want to do it  but there are people that are just naturally better at it.  Encourage and train those but don't punish them by landing everything on them, either.  Spread the love.  And should you, the comms director, be a spokesperson?  In public organisations usually no; in charities OK but a subject specialist is better;

in companies very rarely unless the topic really is about comms. Nobody particularly wants to hear what the 'spin doctor' has to say.

Brief your stakeholders. One of the most important aspects of both positive and negative media coverage is briefing internal audiences and stakeholders before it appears, or as soon as possible after. Don't let the chair of the board be told by someone else that your organisation is all over the Sunday papers. And, if you know that a key stakeholder is going to be asked for comment, consider talking to them in advance so they have the whole picture. The media want the conflict but that doesn't mean you have to hand it to them on a plate. Think about your own staff, too. Make sure they have access to the truth if what is in the papers is selective, or wrong.

Recruitment is key. There is something about knowing what makes a story, and being able to write it, that is difficult to teach. It's a skill that can be acquired through experience but the fast-track is obviously to hire someone who has been a journalist. If you do this, though, you must make sure that they are open to learning all the other skills of being within an organisation's comms team. I once worked with a head of media who I don't think had ever mentally left the newsroom and seemed to be always waiting for the chief executive to trip up so that the big story could be broken. I wanted to say to him, "we are on the same side, you know". I have worked with far more heads of media whose judgment has been vital on how a story will play out and whether it's, on balance, good or bad to take forward a media opportunity (fly-on -the-wall documentaries being a very common discussion.)

Managing reactive and proactive in your press team is challenging. I have always found it difficult to get mostly reactive press teams (eg public sector) to generate positive coverage. There is always too much to do, and generating positive coverage takes so much time – including time for creative thought (which is not easy in a busy office environment and, I think, needs special tactics) and meeting journalists. If you have a big team you can have people dedicated to proactive work, otherwise you might consider bringing in an agency for specific projects or give some of your team real protection to focus on positive, proactive work.

Media relations highlights fault lines in stakeholder dynamics. I was working in the NHS and a coalition of organisations wanted to announce some changes through a press release. The changes would be controversial with the general public so the wording needed to be clear as it would be picked apart by external groups. When the draft press release was sent round to all the coalition partners what then ensued was a week of email wrangling because trying to agree the press release had revealed that the coalition partners weren't really all on the same page.

This is such a familiar story for my public sector colleagues, and it demonstrates how often the comms team become the frontline in negotiating between different parties. It can happen with internal departments disagreeing, too. The lessons are: don't get tied down to a 'launch' date if you suspect that the agreement between the parties isn't secure; try to protect your press officers if you can see that they are in the firing line for trying to find compromise words that others don't like. Take those disagreements out of the press office and resolve them before going public. And, if your level of agreement with the coalition partners is so paper-thin that you are changing individual words in the first paragraph to keep everyone happy, don't think that the cracks won't show the minute the project comes under any public scrutiny. In these circumstances the comms director's advice really is crucial.

## Social media and digital

As I write, a footballer is being panned for retweeting a 'funny' that looked as though it was anti-racist but revealed its nasty true colours with the last line (which I would like to think the footballer hadn't read before retweeting). The chief executive of the football club says he would love to ban all of their players from tweeting, but it just isn't practical.

Social media is a sprawling mess – a potential proliferation of comments about your organisation and your work from people who you don't even know and who you have very little recourse to. But it's also as open to you and your organisation as it is to everyone else. There is no gatekeeper – you can get your message out there in seconds.

As comms director you may find that the people you report to are from the print generation, while the people working for you are from the social media generation. The chief executive knows and worries about this and so becomes too focussed on social media and digital to the detriment of everything else.

Digital comms, primarily by smartphone, will be the core of your practice and will fit into your wider comms strategy but you will also need to build in flex for the unexpected. But be careful not to get pulled too much by what happens on social media – try to be proactive as much as you can.

### Personalisation

Digital allows personalised comms to be easier, so this is what people expect. People have an expectation that comms with them and for them will be targeted and relevant and may be irritated when it isn't.

The difficulty for the board is that direct comms with customers is often split across departments with comms, marketing, customer services etc having an interest and often managing their own direct comms.   The broad overview on how this is done, together with the relative costs and benefits of the various tactics, may need to be taken at board level if a co-operative process isn't already in place. What's key for the comms  director is that although you may not be in charge of the targeted comms to your customers you do need to know the effect that these comms have on your reputation and ability to operate and are able to discuss these with fellow directors. The whole management team needs to remember that getting the comms right is in everyone's best interests – it's not a win/lose situation.

Personalisation isn't just about people as individuals, their name, address and reference numbers – it's also about types of people – grouped with others that have the same central characteristics as them. For instance, Life Members of a charity, people interested in housing for a local council, people who buy lots of cake-baking materials and ingredients for a retailer.

The central question here is: how can we make sure we use what we know about our people to make comms with them more effective?  For you, what your organisation knows about people may be hidden away in databases in another department.  That doesn't mean that it's outside your interest.

Marketing professionals, particularly, segment groups based on their behaviour.  This is good practice for as much of our comms as we can control.   The jargon phrase 'youniverse' refers to the tendency for people to want to be seen as unique personalities and treated as such.

For the comms team this might mean having very

targeted email newsletters, or more than one Facebook page, or clever use of hashtags in Twitter feeds so that people can find what they want from you.

And part of personalisation is letting people control what they receive from you and how. Does your organisation allow them to have their own log-in page with their personal details that they can change? Can they choose which email newsletters they receive?

*Community*
An extension of the theme of personalisation is the increasing movement towards closed online communities for comms. The Facebook and Cambridge Analytica scandal made many people wary about sharing personal information in public spaces online. So, members only Facebook groups, Yammer, Sharepoint and WhatsApp are increasingly popular. The digital space is so vast that people can feel a bit lost, and so they try and create communities – often national or global – with people like them.

How can your organisation be a facilitator for this? Or use these communities to improve your own understanding and engagement? Online chat rooms have been tried, but don't always catch on. Facebook, Reddit or LinkedIn are good places to engage.

The shift to community also means that people may bypass your organisation altogether to find out what they want to know or to talk about your subject. How often do you see questions on networking sites asking things like "What's the best ethical electricity supplier?" "How do I renew my car tax now?" "Don't use Acme Insurance anyone – they messed me about!" People are trusting their own communities more than traditional routes.

*Online champions*

Increasingly organisations are finding that their fans are doing their comms for them. This trend, also called advocacy, is the recognition that the best people to recommend your brand, or information, are the customers themselves. In a commercial world this means telling people to buy from you, in the non-commercial world this might mean that they distribute or highlight your latest bulletins or campaigns.

This has huge advantages for you, because – as we have already discussed – people listen more to their own communities than they do to you. This means, therefore, that you will need to 'feed' your champions, or super-users, or fans or members, so that they share and recommend your information. If you have created forums for them, that helps, but in all cases, you will need good content because it's more likely to be shared.

Part of this trend is the growth in citizen journalism and the plethora of 'digital influencers' – people online that others look at or share. They might be celebrities; they might just be famous in their own little world. They are people who could mention your organisation at any time, and communication teams need to be prepared to respond where necessary, while recognising that they can't respond to everything.

## Content

We have all heard the phrase 'content is king'. Content marketing is a key skill in comms. Essentially it means making sure that your target audiences see and use your information.

The tension here for comms directors is that what people want to read, and are likely to access and share, isn't the same as what people in your organisation want you to say.

We know that the content that gets read and shared is

short, informal, snappy, engaging, interesting, easy-to-read and contains a picture, graphic or video. What you get given to work with is three pages of text using specialist language that may be right for the experts but doesn't work beyond. And then no time or money to develop a video or animation.

"We will deliver a systematic and sustained programme of efficiency and measures for improved effectiveness, translated into sustainable local delivery to ensure the delivery of more stretching centrally derived targets. There will be more emphasis on local ownership and accountability for the identification and delivery of efficiencies." This paragraph made it into 'Pseud's Corner' in *Private Eye* because later in the text the agency (which I won't name because we have all been guilty) pledged to make its communications clear and focused.

The comms director will need to support their team in negotiating with other teams to ensure that content is fit for purpose. Training colleagues to think like a newspaper or broadcast editor and balance what your audience wants and will read with what you want to tell them is crucial. As with the 'perfect' press release – something that everyone internally has signed off but that gets no views or shares is time wasted.

If you want to 'go viral' you have to create content that people want to see (so they don't miss out) and want to share with their network. Comms teams know this, and they have the skills to maximise chances of it happening, but the right balance needs to be struck to make sure that the content is accurate and on-brand as well as shareable. We need to have some understanding and empathy with colleagues from our departments who are sometimes afraid that the comms team will dumb down so much that the content ceases to be credible.

## Transparency

In the strategy and planning chapter I talk about the campaign that the charity Christian Aid started on transparency around the tax that companies pay and in what countries. The public expects much more transparency for organisations now and the internet makes it so much faster and more feasible.

You will no doubt, have conversations internally on what should and shouldn't be published online. Health and safety records, minutes of meetings, financial information, salaries, complaints, entertaining budgets – all these and more will come under pressure.

Arguments in favour of publication include: building trust with people; if we don't someone else will and then we have lost control; we can get it done before legislation or public pressure forces us.

Arguments against include: the risk of people misinterpreting the information; the difficulty of providing context; the risk of a bored journalist picking up some piece of information just to make mischief with it.

What you will need to bear in mind is that public opinion is moving increasingly in favour of transparency so you may as well develop the processes and procedures internally to prepare for transparency even if you don't open up your secrets immediately.

If you do this preparation you will also be able to prepare the necessary context. This is so crucial. If it looks like crime has doubled, the context might be that you have vastly improved levels of reporting. If the figures show that company A's success rates are much worse than company B's, the context might be that company A are very good and specialise in the really difficult projects, so their success rates are lower.

Transparency is not the holy grail. It is not a positive end in itself. The increase of understanding and trust is a positive end, and transparency is a part of this but needs context.

## Sign-off

We can't end a chapter on media and social media without tackling the tricky area of sign-off. Danny Baker lost his job on BBC Radio Five Live for a very unwise tweet when a Royal baby was born. I am not sure if he showed anyone else that tweet before he pressed send, but if he had I think he would still be in a job.

For press releases it's fairly straightforward – you will probably have a set process for sign-off that includes the person who is being quoted and the senior director in charge of that area. In some places the chief executive sees everything. If you are the chief exec or the senior director I would advise that you comment on factual accuracy mostly, and anything that might upset a stakeholder, and that you give the press team fairly free rein with paragraph one, which is the 'top line' that is being used to catch the attention of the media.

Social media is more difficult because speed is very important, and a natural voice is essential.

And it's difficult to tell your chief executive that they should ensure someone reads their tweets before sending them when a President of the United States,in the shape of Donald Trump, doesn't follow this rule!

If you can, advocate for a rule that nobody should tweet without someone else reading it, and for contentious subjects that should be a senior colleague. A sign-off policy for social media that requires the chief executive to see everything before it goes out would be unusually cumbersome but ensure that the decision can be escalated if the digital team have concerns.

## Conclusion

The comms job is not just responding to 'always on' it's responding to 'always on, everywhere'.

How can you control the organisation's reputation when there are so many more channels and mentions? You can't. In some ways organisations have to accept that they cannot protect their brand in the way that they might have done in the past but you increase the danger if you opt out of trying or attempt to ignore the media and social media. Developing champions and having accurate and shareable content is useful. Creating 'fans' of your content is one possible mitigation for the negative content, as is ensuring that your content is useful and easily shareable. There may be negative mentions but try to ensure that you empower people to create lots of positive mentions, too.

Chapter Two

# Internal Communications

- **What are the pitfalls that the directors need to look out for with staff comms?**
- **Which is the most under-valued group of staff?**
- **How to empower staff to be champions.**

The Government had decided to merge two big regulators and I was advising the chair of the new shadow organisation. As I always do in these situations, I warned her to be really careful with her language so that the she didn't alienate some of the staff who were feeling side-lined in the merger. So, my heart sank as she described them (they were inspectors) in a media interview as the people who "run their fingers round the toilet bowl". Needless to say, they weren't chuffed by this description. It became a morbid joke across the organisation and the quality team even produced a spoof 'colour chart' (I won't go into detail) to help the inspectors.  As you would expect, it was uphill from then on for the new chair and this set of staff.

Internal, or staff, comms, is one of the subjects in our repertoire that has so many good books written about it you could fill a bookshop. So, I will keep this chapter short and focus on what's helpful for the senior team.

As directors, and particularly as chief executive, your most powerful and useful contribution to internal comms will be to live, breathe and evangelise our old favourite adage "actions speak louder than words".

You have all the different channels pumping out news, stories and information, but the actions of the top team shout ten times louder than the nice words crafted by the comms team for the newsletter.

Time and time again I have seen chief executives get the process for engagement and consultation right – because that's what they know they have to do – and then destroy all the goodwill with a loose comment or action. It happens so often that I think it's worth warning the key senior people in advance to be really careful about what they say and do because it will be read through very critical lenses, particularly during periods of stress.

If it's a contentious situation such as reorganisation or a merger don't forget that the senior people involved will, themselves, be stressed. But the stress for them will get much worse if they trip themselves up with injudicious actions and your job is to try and stop them from making it worse for everyone.

For the comms director your responsibilities fall into two categories: your personal advice to the senior leadership team and ensuring your team provide a good internal comms service.

### Advising your leadership team

Let's look first at how the comms director works with the leadership team. You are likely to need to be influential at times when the organisation is launching new initiatives or dealing with something difficult. You will want to see that the process has the right level of engagement with staff and the messaging is balanced.

At NHS England I remember working on the comms for a very complex reorganisation of part of the NHS. It had been a difficult year all round for this large national division. They knew there was going to be drastic downsizing across the country, but reorganisations elsewhere meant their situation hadn't been addressed yet. The new management team came in and it looked like they would get some decisions. The staff had their own dedicated email newsletter telling them the updates on how the reorganisation plans were going for their division. But time after time they were promised a decision that failed to materialise. They steeled themselves for the key dates – would they have a job? Could they book a holiday? And the key dates went past with just another excuse about delays. It almost didn't matter what the nice words in the newsletter said, the staff learnt to expect disappointment.

And on the other side of this newsletter was a comms team who were desperately pleading with the management team not to promise new dates for decisions. "But there really will be a decision this time – the chief executive has said so," we were told. And so we promised. And again, it wasn't delivered. It was a credit to the staff in this division that they did any work at all given the way they were treated.

Remember that comms professionals often see people issues differently from their colleagues. Internal comms is an area where your skills, instincts and outlook are really valuable, and could prevent the organisation making costly mistakes in handling. You will no doubt be working with the senior HR professionals, and hopefully they, too, will have this outlook although they will also be weighing up the legal and trade union issues, too. Sadly, you might also be working with some old-school managers who don't see the value of creative internal comms because, while they might say the right things, their actions show they secretly still believe in command and control.

So, make sure your voice is heard around the senior management team table. And if you are the chief executive, this might be an area where the scary 'gut feel' of the comms director needs to be sought and listened to.

Engagement is the word you will read in all the books on change management. Try to ensure that there is sufficient engagement to give the staff the chance to influence what happens and feel ownership of the result. However, be careful to make sure that you aren't designing engagement just because you know it's supposed to happen, but not actually giving the staff any real power over what happens or taking account of what is said.

Patronising, meaningless engagement will waste everybody's time and build resentment. Where consultation is a legal requirement make sure that the staff have the context for what is happening so that they can offer alternative solutions that meet the objectives. If it's genuinely about cost-cutting, be honest and say so.

Try to ensure that there is a senior person visibly leading the project. Don't let your colleagues hide behind phrases like, "The management team have decided..." This is obviously easier for something positive like the consultation on the new business strategy, but more difficult if you are down-sizing. Then make sure the senior person sets the right tone, is seen at the right events or offices and responds correctly to the suggestions and comments that are sent to them. Actions speaking louder than words.

And make sure that all the right people are supported. I have been surprised by the number of times that change projects under-cater for the managers who are one or two levels below the top and in charge of trying to keep the show on the road while still worrying about their own jobs. In fact, I have found that this group, often called the "squeezed middle" receive less of the chief executive's attention routinely.   These are the people who the staff at the frontline will get their information from.  Yes, you will be sending out the messages from head office, and perhaps there will be some events, but the middle managers will be the interpreters.  If your organisation does a staff attitude survey you will often be able to clearly identify this group and what they are feeling.  They need their own dedicated comms – perhaps through a regular teleconference, or a meeting. They need the specific support and encouragement of whoever is leading the project and you might spot that this isn't happening because everyone is intent on what's happening at the very front line.

As comms director, while your team will probably be preparing the regular comms materials, the context that you have means that you will probably need to advise on messaging for these higher profile projects. It really does save time and energy if you get these right.

You may be fortunate and be working with excellent communicators, but in general, the tendency of the project leader will be to use messaging that is obscure and/or over positive.   "We are looking to maximise the efficiency levels of our operations, looking at a number of factors including locations, resource-levels, costs and performance metrics." What does this mean?  Cutting offices?  Cutting people? Cutting the people that don't perform well?

Another example: "our priority is our staff and we will make every effort to ensure their safety and well-being." Excellent, so no job cuts then.

As with all comms plans, you have hopefully set out your overall strategy and this might include ensuring that people understand both the difficult economic situation, and how they can contribute to the plans.  Make sure the messaging is clear and honest. This doesn't necessarily mean that you declare everything – there are many twists and turns in projects such as these which mean you can't - it just means that what you do say is straightforward and true. You will need to give the right amount of context, and make sure that you spell out next steps and how people can feedback or ask questions (if you have made this option available).

## Running your internal communications service
You may have a person or team responsible for internal comms. Hopefully they will also have a good relationship with the senior people in the organisation that they need to work with – usually the director of operations and the director of HR.

It is really important to ensure that internal comms in your organisation fits in with your overall comms strategy and delivers efficiently. Your staff are a very influential stakeholder, as well as being the core of your delivery.

You will have specific internal comms objectives that, probably, your head of internal comms has written. However, you will also need to ensure that the staff are properly regarded as key communicators for the rest of your comms. Think of the number of stakeholders – customers, pressure groups, government links – that deal directly with your staff. Make sure that your own staff have the information they need to be positive influencers. Don't put them in the position of not already knowing information that is sent routinely to stakeholders. They are your biggest asset as communicators and should be empowered to be so.

In overseeing whether you have an efficient internal comms operation, you are probably looking at the quality of the channels, the effectiveness of the targeting, the number of different ways that people can find things out, the opportunities for engagement and the level and quantity of information that is given out.

Look out for these risks:

• ***Is your organisation over-reliant on one channel?*** Such as the weekly email?  It's easy for everyone to think that because something has been said in the weekly email that's the communication done. Monitoring the figures for who opens them will show whether they are having any cut-through.

• ***Are you under-communicating on the big issues?*** Is your weekly email full of news about the fire safety training, but silent on what happened at the board meeting, or the pay review meeting?

• ***Are you repetitive on the things that count?*** One of the big mistakes with internal comms is that we say things once and think that's the job done.  As with using more than one channel, we need to make sure that we repeat information that really needs to sink in.

• ***Are you silent when there is nothing to say?*** This is a question for the difficult projects, not the routine comms.  A project that is happening over a long period of time may not be top of the list for the senior team or the comms team but is, perhaps, occupying every waking thought of the people whose jobs are at risk.  In these circumstances people draw on every rumour or scrap of news to fill the gap.  You might want to make sure that you give updates even when there isn't much to say.

## Conclusion

There is no shortage of advice on this subject because it is so closely linked to the overall performance of your organisation. Companies succeed and fail on the basis of how they engage and empower their own staff. Make sure that you use your position at the top of the organisation to influence how things are done as much as what is said. This is where your intervention could make a big difference.

Chapter Three

# Strategy and Planning

- **How do you turn 'very busy' into 'very effective'?**
- **How do you decide what not to do?**
- **Is your comms strategy lost in a dark corner of the shared drive?**

I arrived at work at 9am and the first task was breakfast in the staff canteen. This took about half-an-hour. Then back to the office to check if had received any emails and when the answer was no I would start reading the day's papers. Perhaps about 10.30 I would phone someone or do some research on the internet for a paper that had to be submitted in a month's time, and I would keep this going until lunch-time – a wonderful, full-hour event with plenty of chat. Afternoon would hopefully include a meeting of some sort but would otherwise be waiting for an email to come in and doing lots of catching up (gossiping) with other colleagues in the team.

This was the one time in my life when I didn't have enough to do as a communications manager. (It was strangely stressful). Every other time the job has been full-on, too much to do, feeling guilty at what you can't do, worrying about deadlines, getting a buzz out of being active, but always trying to fit a quart into a pint pot.

This is one of the roles of good strategy and planning: not just deciding what to do but deciding what not to do (the more difficult bit). As a good comms director you need to do this for yourself, but – more importantly – you need to do it for your team and for your organisation. There is too much wasted activity in our field.

As a chief executive it's very easy to ask the director for a comms strategy and then have little understanding of what should be in it. All your comms should be handled strategically, and this chapter shows you what that means. Ideally this would have been the first chapter and the beginning of your thinking, but although absolutely vital, I concede that it's not the most interesting place to start.

In this chapter I have split this subject into four areas:
1. How to plan strategically
2. The organisation's comms strategy
3. Working strategically on everything you do
4. Making sure your messaging across lots of projects is planned and consistent.


## 1. How to plan strategically

Strategic comms is an under-recognised skill in our profession. You can get too far without any experience or knowledge of how to do it whatsoever. This wouldn't be allowed in lots of other professions and I feel sad every time I witness it happening in ours.

I have had conversations with people who are heading off for interviews for director jobs and have taken me to one side and asked me what strategic comms is. These people have gone on to be brilliant (in most cases) – it's the discipline they were lacking not the ability to do it.

Working strategically has several benefits:
- It stops us just using the email inbox to dictate our activity.
- It stops us from just using our intuition to decide

what to do.
- It makes us continue with a plan of messaging and dialogue much longer than we might otherwise, and this means it has a chance of actually influencing behaviour and opinion.
- It allows us to properly defend the things that we aren't going to do and fend off 'bright ideas'.
- It makes sure everyone is on the same page so they can all target their activity.
- It brings on board the people whose brains work better with a plan.

In the mental health sector, for example, there has been a long-running attempt to reduce the stigma associated with having mental illness. From a slow start 25 years ago, it is now a well-researched and well-delivered campaign across the sector. One of the reasons I first worked in comms in mental health was because I felt that my skills in changing public behaviour could improve the well-being of people who were suffering not only from a debilitating mental illness, but also the awful public attitudes towards them because of their diagnosis. Things have got a lot better but there is a long way to go.

So, what is strategic comms? Well the core of the Chartered Institute of Public Relations' definition of public relations (a title I prefer, by the way, if it hadn't been hijacked to refer to selling stories to the media) is "the planned and sustained effort to establish and maintain goodwill and mutual understanding between an organisation and its publics."

Working strategically means always keeping in mind the long-term goal(s), being realistic about what can be achieved and being relentless in trying to achieve it.

I usually use a simple question framework to help people think through the comms strategy for a particular task.

1. Objectives
a. What are our goals? (organisation goals, not comms team goals)

2. Stakeholders
a. Who can help us to achieve these goals?
b. Who can stop us achieving these goals?
c. Of these, which have the most capacity to help/harm?

3. Analysis
a. What do they think/do/believe at the moment?
b. What are the gaps in their knowledge?
c. What do we want them to know/believe/understand?
d. What is our relationship like with them at the moment?
e. What would we like it to be?

4. Action plan
a. What do we need to do to get us from now, to what we want?
b. Who is going to do what?
c. How are we going to review and update this plan?

This framework can be used to facilitate discussion with the team who need the comms strategy. For example, the senior leadership team, the policy team or the operations team.

### Objective
It is important to set this correctly otherwise it is then difficult to get the right prioritisation of stakeholders. It should be an organisational goal, which has – hopefully – already been

decided in a strategic fashion. So, you can have a goal which is "reduce water use" if the operations team have already established that this is one of their priorities, and this is a goal that will help them hit their targets. You can have a goal which is "reduce staff costs by 30% in the operations division" if the organisation has already strategically decided that this is what it needs to do.

The goal isn't usually just a comms team goal, such as "make a new corporate video." And it especially isn't this when it's just been dictated to you by the person in charge of the project . "Make us a video, I notice that our competitors all have them and I want everyone to know about this new project." In this case, a conversation is required on what this manager wants to achieve and what are the best ways to achieve it. A video might be right, but it needs to be thought through and researched. Perhaps the target audience would be more likely to use a podcast that can be listened to in the car.

When you have your goal you may need to set a few sub-goals to ensure that you are on track. For example, within a certain budget, or within the overall messaging framework of your organisation, or which reinforces other objectives of your organisation. So, for example, "reduce staff costs by 30%..." might have a sub-goal of "maximising the use of the new Sharepoint platform for comms" or it might say "ensuring safety and business continuity".

### *Stakeholders*
Once you have your overall goal, the step is to work out who – inside and outside your organisation – you need on board to get you there. My preference for doing this piece of thinking is to get the top people of the project into a room to discuss the stakeholder mapping. They know their

stakeholders best and the comms specialists can facilitate a discussion that takes them through the questions above (usually just the first few). The richness of the conversation, and your questioning, will have a massive value in itself.

What you need to do is get them to identify in increasing detail who can influence your progress towards your goal.

Example stakeholders would therefore include other organisations, relevant media, politicians, pressure groups, local government, customers and users, commentators and possibly large swathes of people such as "general public" or "citizens".

While you are doing this, you are trying to get a sense of which have the greatest influence. Which organisation, or person, has the power to make a final decision? Who releases the finance? Who could make such a noise that your reputation could be damaged so much you would have to stop?

And if they have high influence you will need to do more unpacking of that group. So, for example, you might unpack the category for pressure groups, by deciding that Green Action Now is not very influential even though they have a lot of members, but Don't Fry our Future is very powerful because of their connections and their ability to mobilise quickly.

When looking at this you are looking at who can hinder your progress towards the goal as well as who can accelerate it, and this may require some lateral thinking because sometimes they are less vocal and less obvious. For example, a stakeholder who isn't very interested in your subject but is very powerful would score higher than a public interest group who are passionately interested in your goal but don't have a lot of sway.

For some stakeholders you will need to break the

group right down into key individuals, especially if there is a variety of opinions or behaviours about your goal within the stakeholder group. So, if the chairman of a stakeholder organisation is a fan of yours but the Director of Strategy isn't, you may need a different approach for each. Equally you might find that relations at the top of the stakeholder organisation are good, but at regional level they are generally antagonistic.

For people who are less interested but powerful, you may need to map around them to find the people that influence that group or person. So, for a politician for example, they are very responsive to media coverage and public opinion. You may have to influence their influencers if it's difficult to get to them directly.

As you continue your discussions you will need to move the stakeholders into a rough priority order. Hopefully your experts around the table will do this, and the comms director's role is to keep them focussed on who can really make a difference – not just trot out who are the loudest voices. You will often find that this is when the penny drops for them that they will need to be doing most of the comms themselves, probably in one-to-ones with the powerful people.

So, your mapping will have at the core people, or groups, who have a lot of ability to influence whether you get to your goal, moving outwards until you get to people who you are not going to include in your strategy at all because you don't want to waste effort (or their time).

You may want to use a framework for this mapping and prioritisation. There are plenty available in textbooks and on the internet. However, I find that it's actually the discussion, with the interventions and questioning of the comms professional, that is the most valuable part of the mapping exercise and if you just give the project team a 'power/influence' matrix to fill in they will produce a very nice powerpoint slide that, in practice, hardly influences the team's behaviour at all.

### Analysis

The next task is to make sure you really understand your top stakeholders. What do you know about where they stand on your issue already? And can you trust what the team say they think? "All the residents think we shouldn't sell" says the relevant director. Is this true? Perhaps lots of the residents would be secretly quite pleased if you sold but aren't particularly vocal in saying so. At this stage decide whether you need some opinion research, or desk research to establish what people think. Don't head off on your strategy in the wrong direction from the very first point.

You will also need to map what forms of comms you already have with these people and groups. Does your organisation have regular meetings with them? Do they subscribe to your newsletter? Do they have preferred channels of comms? Properly understanding the important stakeholders is so valuable at this stage. And a key lesson here is to get as much proper evidence as you can so that you can triangulate what instinct and gut feeling is telling you and your advisors. This doesn't always mean commissioning research – it sometimes means just asking within your own organisation what they know. The customer services team or the field office might give you some very useful insights.

The next stage of the analysis section is to discuss where you would like your relationship with these stakeholders to be. What would you like them to know? How would you like them to behave? What do you want them to do?

This is where you are trying to set realistic targets for the key stakeholders. The discussion here needs to move backwards from the ideal world into the real world. "I want everyone to agree to this plan and stop complaining," might be what your team would love to happen but is it realistic? If a 180-degree opinion shift is required, is that possible? If so, how much effort is required to get there? If not, what is your plan B?

### *Action plan*
Once you have finished the analysis and decided what you want to achieve (realistically) you move on to the action plan. When you are preparing the plan, remember that it is likely that the really key activities are not done by the comms team, but by the leading people in the relevant team who either are, or need to be, talking directly to the most influential people. Part of your job is to help them prioritise their time and to ensure that there is enough repeat activity with the really key people. Quite often we prioritise activity by who is shouting loudest. They may not be the most influential people or groups. They need proper engagement, but not at the expense of perhaps quieter but much more influential people.

So, your action plan is likely to include:

### *a) Research*
This might include any opinion research that you need so you fully understand the stakeholders. Or, research to help you set benchmarks on opinion and behaviour so that you can see over time how successful you are and which activities are working and which aren't. (There is more about this in the research and evaluation chapter)

### *b) Strategy*
When you have looked at the analysis and before you get into

the detail you will need to decide what kind of approach you are going to use. This is a summary of the thinking behind your approach and why you think it will work. For example, part of your strategy might be, "The public trust scientists, therefore our strategy will be to empower our scientists to be our key communicators."

*c) Methods*

Here you are choosing how to communicate with each of the stakeholders you have identified. The choices here extend from the very personal – a one-to-one meeting – to mass, global comms such as your website. Options are likely to fall into these categories:

- personal contact: one-to-one meetings, phone calls, teleconferences
- personal emails, group emails, newsletter
- noticeboard material, posters
- media work
- social media comments or dedicated pages
- videos, podcasts
- information on your website, or dedicated pages or a dedicated website
- printed materials – newsletters, leaflets
- champions, fan clubs, member schemes
- public meetings, roadshows, exhibitions
- information phone line
- consultations – formal or informal, surveys
- paid-for advertising, direct mail, door drops, POS material
- competitions
- campaigns
- celebrity endorsements
- apps for smartphones

- petitions
- merchandising (car air freshener with "watch your speed" on).

When choosing channels, think about how credible the channel is. For example, charities have internal struggles because they know lots of supporters hate being phoned at home, but also lots of them increase their giving when they are phoned. On balance, do telephone campaigns harm your reputation so much that the income gains are not worth it, or is the money it brings in just too valuable and worth the losses?

At the same time, you sometimes have to use channels that some people don't like, but this can be explained. The Green Party had struggled for years with the dilemma that leafletting homes is a very effective way to campaign but risks wasting a lot of paper. One way it responded was to make a point of  asking people for an email address and phone number so that they could reduce the use of leaflets.

Individuals, too, have levels of credibility based on all sorts of criteria. It shouldn't be true, but it is true that people with regional accents come across better than people with accents perceived as 'posh'. Why do you think so many call centres are based in the north-east and in Scotland? University comms teams prefer to use professors and subject specialists for interviews, transport companies will use a front-line specialist in a hard-hat and a dayglo jacket wherever possible for media work and public consultations. Government ministers have found their credibility ratings falling hugely over recent decades so departments find they can have more impact on behaviour change if they work with respected charities.

Some honesty might be necessary here for your own

senior team. The operations director who is widely known and hated for closing down D division, may not be the best person to put on stage at the staff conference to talk about the new vision however much he wants to. The director of R&D who has an infectious enthusiasm for the products might not in theory be the right person to speak on the media, but she comes across so well that you find your team and the media love her.

When planning the 'how' you need to make sure that each stakeholder has sufficient engagement to properly impact on their understanding of your issues. This means repeating messages, repeating engagement, listening, responding to their questions and comments and so on until you get where you need to be. How many times have we heard from our colleagues in other departments "I told them. So, why are they still getting it wrong?" Your colleagues may have tried hard to communicate but it's often the case that 'they' were told once, in a long email which they probably didn't read, and weren't interested in, and there has been little or no shift in their understanding or behaviour. Good comms advice will ratchet up hammering home the message or keeping the dialogue open. This means creating lots of opportunities to see the messaging and lots of clever tactics to get people to engage with it. If people are interested in the message and want to know the information you will need less repeats. If it's something they aren't particularly looking out for, you will need to come at them from as many angles as you can – getting a mix of, perhaps, the media work, the email approaches and the social media coverage.

If you are not an experienced comms professional you may be surprised by just how valuable even straightforward comms planning can be. The Environment Agency learned this when its flood risk experts, for the best of motives, pretty much imposed a new flood management scheme on a community. It was the right scheme and the public were at real risk, but insufficient attention to public relations meant it was opposed by local people, went to judicial review and was held up for many years.

On the opposite bank of the same estuary a little later the team carried out consultation with the public for a similar scheme and it was established with public support, built and working in a couple of years, saving the flood management team money and time, and protecting the public – the core mission of the Agency.

### d) Who in your own organisation will be doing what?
The action plan needs to be clear about responsibilities. Spell out the specific tasks, responsibilities and accountabilities.

### e) Messaging
This phrase has its critics because it implies a one-way form of communication, but I have found that people are greatly helped by having a messaging framework. The messaging framework will be informed by what your key stakeholders know, think and believe already and which gaps or inaccuracies you need to fill or correct.

For example, I helped a charity with a messaging framework that brought out the extent of the social and community work that they did. Their supporters associated them with the arts and performances and their community arts projects were under-recognised. The messaging framework therefore needed to address this by making sure that the key statements they used about themselves included their community work.

So, the time you spend properly understanding where your stakeholders are now is key here. What are their values, preconceptions, information needs?

Resist the temptation to make your messaging all about what you want to say, and overlook what people want or need to hear. A good example of this is when I was a speaker on the subject of global poverty. I wanted to tell people that global poverty could and should be ended, but they often wouldn't 'hear' or assimilate this message because they had preconceptions that money given to charities is wasted or lost in corrupt governance systems overseas. So, I found I had to speak directly about corruption and address the issues that were stopping people hearing the rest. You will have similar unwelcome, issues to address in your own messaging, don't skirt round them and leave the 'elephant in the room' bellowing across your rosy prose. Try to resist letting others pressure you to polish the messaging until has such an unrealistic glow that nobody would believe it. Yes, you want a positive topline, but make sure it is true, potentially believable (even if it isn't understood at the moment) and straightforward (easy to comprehend). The skilled wordsmiths in your team will be valuable in making sure that the messages are easy to express, short and memorable. Then they have a chance of being used!

You may also need to be the champion for emotions and empathy. Sometimes when our messaging is researched, crafted and emailed around for comments it loses the human quality that helps people to engage with it.

Good public speakers know that it's the story of how little Emily was saved by the firefighters that will be remembered, not the correct facts and figures on fire safety and response. Make sure you keep the heart in your messaging.

### f) Timetable
Your plan will need to be realistic and set within the time

frames of the project. Map out the main deadlines and make sure that you allow enough lead up time for the stakeholder work. Remember that telling people something once does not mean that they understand or believe it. If this was true, the advertising industry would be decimated. As mentioned before, your timetable should allow the right amount of time for the attitude and behaviour shifts that you are seeking, and this is often longer than most people would think.

When I worked for the international development charity Christian Aid in 2008, we started a campaign for companies to be more transparent about their tax payments. The argument was that if companies paid proper levels of tax in developing countries this would fund social services such as health and education. The first step in the campaign was just to get companies to show what they paid in each country - transparency. At the time it seemed like a very niche campaign. It was complicated, a bit boring and difficult for supporters to get excited about, but we kept going. Six years later, accountancy firm Ernst and Young sponsored a 30-page supplement in the Financial Times on exactly this subject with advice on how to do it. And now, in 2019, transparency and tax avoidance and evasion are firmly on the public agenda. So, planning timetables need to allow enough time for awareness to increase and attitudes to shift.

## g) Project management

How are you going to keep everyone on track with the comms strategy? Identify your project leader and perhaps project sponsor (which might be the comms director) and whether you will have regular meetings to make sure that all the parts of the plan are on track. If your colleagues in the relevant business unit are also carrying out some of the comms (for instance with individual key stakeholders) you have an even greater need for the meetings where you bring people together to find out what the progress is and what people are saying. This is where you will decide if you need to introduce new activities or change the messaging.

## h) Evaluation and review

This is discussed in more detail in a later chapter. Suffice it to say here that it's useful to identify in advance your success criteria, and your methods of knowing how much progress you are making. Sometimes this is conveniently very quantifiable (how many people signed up for a scheme) but often it isn't and will need either some research, or perhaps a peer review approach (where the project is evaluated by the opinions of trusted people on its success).

## i) Actions speak louder than words

It is important to add some thoughts in this chapter about this vastly underrated truth. In nearly every training session that I do on comms I mention this. It's a bland, twee, familiar, idealistic phrase seen on tea-towels across the world. But it is the petrol that will either fuel your comms plan into over-drive or bring it down in flames. It is so powerful. "Your views are important to us" says the blurb, but if there is no response, or evidence of any of the views being taken into account then the words are meaningless.

When I worked at 10 Downing Street on comms for public sector reform, we arranged for the Prime Minister to turn up without advance publicity at key staff conferences. He gave a short speech and took questions and because there were no media there, the audience group knew that the only value of the visit was for their benefit. The words 'we value public sector staff' were being demonstrated by the action of the Prime Minister taking time to visit you and your conference and answer your questions. Contrast this with the criticism levelled at Boris Johnson in October 2019 he visited a hospital with a TV crew. An angry father, Omar Salem, challenged him on his party's record on the NHS and accused him of just visiting 'for a press opportunity.'

So, the actions need to be back up the messaging and the rhetoric, and they also need to be consistent with your organisation's values. When putting together your action plan make sure you think (and feel) like a human being. If your project is contentious how are you going to support people who might be upset at the consultation meeting? If your organisation is able to engage with the whole person, emotions and feelings, not just thoughts and beliefs, your activities will be much more effective. There is a reason why the phrase 'winning hearts and minds' puts 'hearts' first.

In 2013 I worked on the independent scrutiny of the NHS complaints process for the Clwyd Hart review. One of the key findings was that it seemed the complaints process didn't account for and allow for the depth of people's feelings when something goes wrong. It might have been efficient, but it was often not empathetic.


## 2. Organisational strategy

The comms manager from one of the organisations in my region rings me. "The board have asked me to write a comms strategy. Can you send me someone else's so I can see what headings they have used and write my own version?" This is a short version of a very frequent conversation when I was a regional comms manager. It's strange, isn't it, that even seasoned comms professionals resort to Google when the Board wants an overarching strategy. There are a few questions to ask or think about when you are asked for this

(or if you are doing the asking.)

What do you think the Board really wants and why? And, if you are the comms director, what do you, yourself, want to achieve through it?

It is a good discipline to have an over-arching comms strategy – particularly to fit in with a business planning process. And it's a good discipline for the comms department to have one so the team know what the priorities are. So, whether you are asked to do one or not by the Board, they are a good idea – but don't set your expectations too high on what they will achieve and measure the effort you put into them accordingly.

The plans can differ greatly depending on how your board work, what's happened in the past, whether you need this document to drive the comms team, how much the organisation truly understands about itself and how much investment it is willing to put into comms (financially and in time).

However, here are some general pointers to help you build your own approach.

You can follow a fairly similar pattern to the structure in 1) above. But these overarching, plans are often much more discursive. A typical organisation-wide strategy will have:

- A commentary on the organisation's purpose and the context in which it sits economically, socially and politically.
- A description of the organisation's goals and priorities. Whatever you decide to write, you must make sure that your strategy is built around the  priorities. If these are expressed in an annual or five-year business plan or vision or mission statement, then use these.  If your organisation doesn't have these, and just carries on day-by-day as it has always done,

you may have to write them yourself. But don't miss them out altogether.

- What, generally, the specific issues are for its reputation and relationships. What clients think, what pressure groups think, what political pressures exist.
- Who the main stakeholder groups are and a commentary on their attitudes, impact and your engagement with them.
- A description of your existing and planned comms channels and a discussion of any issues or plans (for example a new website).
- You may have a timetable and action plan, but it can usually only be very high level. However, you need to give assurance that more detailed action plans exist and are common practice.
- If the strategy is for consultation, or for the Board, add in any questions you have. If it's for your board, it always helps them if they know what feedback you would like. This doesn't mean that they won't comment on other parts of the strategy, but it is a good opportunity for you to ask them to focus on the things you would most value input on. Examples might include their perception of where you stand with certain stakeholders – board members often have a very good view of these.

My experience is that board-level strategies are useful for educating their readers as much as for setting priorities. It is your chance to land some key messages yourself with your colleagues. They also don't get a huge amount of comment or engagement from the board – they exist to reassure the board that you are on-top of the job. They also suffer from only getting looked at when they are first written and then languishing in a dark corner of the shared drive. Although this sounds like a waste of your time, it isn't surprising as they are often too big and global to really drive your activity on a day-to-day basis. The thought processes going into them are important, the reassurance for the board is important and the feedback you get is important for you and your team. After that you are better to apply your strategic and planning skills to the specific projects.

### 3. Working strategically all the time
It is fairly easy and tempting to do the job unstrategically. You get ad-hoc requests from people for comments, press releases, events. You have a bright idea for something that you put in place, you see someone else's website and decide you want to overhaul your own. A salesperson persuades you to buy some mugs with your strapline on. You get lots of letters from customers about an issue, so you write some answers. You have some regular activities such as blogs and email newsletters that keep you all busy. It can be very time-consuming and rewarding, but ultimately less productive than it should be for the effort you are putting in.

Try to encourage your colleagues and your team to always think strategically. How can they reinforce the headline messaging? How can they ensure you prioritise key stakeholders? Are they thinking about what can realistically be achieved? Is there a proper value to the organisation for what they are doing? Most specifically, try to stop people from one-off contacts with stakeholders, or one-off messages, or one-off activities for an internal team that will have no lasting value with their stakeholder groups.

Examples would be attending the industry set-piece event and making a one-off decision about what your display should be that isn't based on any other activity or messaging throughout the year. Or, as a campaigning charity, asking your supporters to email their MP about an issue that you haven't previously been particularly engaged with and don't have the resources to research sufficiently. Or writing an article by-lined for your chair for a respected journal without giving any thought to your main comms strategy for the main messages.

Your team will be given specific jobs to do but they should always set them in the wider strategy. I was working as a consultant for a charity who wanted me to think about a new approach to their annual reporting and then write the necessary annual reports. It would have been easy to just write a nice description of everything they had done that year, ask the directors to give me some words, and find some nice pictures.

However, that would not have been a strategic approach. The report was going to their donors and influential stakeholders. So, I needed to know what, ideally, they wanted those people to know. For this, I needed to know what they were trying to achieve as an organisation and what messaging about them needed to be reinforced to make this happen. They wanted to build awareness and uptake of a new service they launched last year so that got a lot of space. They wanted to encourage more donations from a particular type of donors so we highlighted lots of successes from that type of funding. And they wanted to counter some attitudes among their most influential supporters, so we included lots of positive messaging about that. Hopefully, this hit the buttons that they needed to hit. Ideally, this wouldn't be the only method they used to hit these buttons. This type of approach isn't rocket science, but it's surprising how often it gets ignored.

## 4. Cross-organisational planning

How do you make sure that all the activities from your organisation, and all the messaging, and all the activity is co-ordinated on a day-to-day basis? How do you keep an eye on how you are delivering your key messages over time? In theory you need a planning mechanism for your comms that takes in everything. In practice I have never seen one work very well.

When I was at 10 Downing Street we worked with the Government departments who were concentrating on delivery of public services to support effective planning tools. The departments had put some of their best people onto trying to develop the spreadsheets, diaries and schedules that would make sure that announcements didn't clash and that main messages were repeated.

At Number 10 itself one of the key roles in the comms team was the man who controlled The Grid. This was like air-traffic control for government comms. Every announcement from every department had to have its place on the grid, together with its key messaging. The Gridmeister would scour the papers every day hoping that he wouldn't find an announcement that he didn't know about in advance.

I have tried various methods with the teams I have managed. At one place we had mega-planning sessions where we got everyone together and let loose with the sticky-notes, wallpaper and pens. I have also tried designating one, very organised and detail-loving, person to be in charge of the master-spreadsheet. I haven't tried using an agency who specialise in this, but I know others who have and they find they pay for lots of complicated, colour-coded spreadsheets.

And I worked with one client that had absolutely no cross-organisational planning mechanism at all, and no restriction on when each individual team could say what it wanted on its very own social media feeds and email cascades. On the day of a major political landslide that shocked the nation they were announcing a new fun and friendly fundraising initiative. It didn't look great. (To their credit they have improved since.) The net conclusion of all this is that is really isn't easy, but there is value in trying to find a solution that works for you and your team. At the very least you need an event diary to ensure that you don't have clashes. At the most you can map messaging and stakeholder approaches onto this. Good luck!

## Conclusion

Good strategic thinking is the difference between being very busy and being very effective. If you are not a strategic person yourself, make use of the questioning framework to keep your comms focussed on the main priorities. If you are a strategic person, don't underestimate how difficult some people find this and try to make your thinking accessible. Training in strategy and planning from an early stage will be invaluable.

## Chapter Four

# Stakeholder Management

- **Can stakeholder relations realistically be 'managed'?**
- **Is stakeholder relations the most important part of comms planning?**
- **How do you make public consultations effective?**

When I first worked in Government communications it was fairly straightforward. The policy officials would write the policy. The comms team would get it typeset and printed. The door of the Government department would be opened briefly while the documents were let out for delivery to the country. The press office would issue the announcement and then it was mostly just left to happen. Occasionally the policy officials might peep out through the window to see if anyone was implementing what they had written. If not, they would write some more.

And then people started to think that being responsible for delivery was also important, and 'stakeholder relations' arrived. There was a period at the turn of the century when the practice of stakeholder management gripped Government departments. The departments for health and education were particularly good at it. They brought teachers, doctors and other professionals into the departments to help shape policy and be part of rolling it out effectively. Senior jobs which had previously been offered to career civil servants were offered to people from the field. Reference groups were formed, and stakeholder maps were everywhere. The pendulum did eventually swing a little too far the other way but generally it was a very healthy opening up of Government.

This was the age of deference – when we mostly trusted our governments, public institutions, charities and businesses to do the right thing. The death of deference, and the assumption that institutions are probably hiding something, means we have to work much more proactively with stakeholders to keep our licence to operate.

In 2008 when I was Director of Comms, User and Public Involvement at the Commission for Social Care Inspection we introduced a user-friendly star-rating system for care homes. This made life easy for people using services to choose their services, but it had serious implications for the people running the services. Weaknesses that could be hidden away in an inspection report become much clearer when the service is rated one-star, or 'poor'. So, we had an extensive consultation and dialogue process with care services companies to underpin the delivery and make sure that it was clear to everyone that we want to support services to reach three stars, the top rating. We then made sure that the messaging at launch stressed that 70% of services are in the two- and three-star categories, meaning they are good or excellent.

Getting the stakeholder relations right can be the difference between success and failure. The actual practice of mapping stakeholders and working out a stakeholder relations strategy is described in detail in the strategy and planning chapter, so this chapter is a brief look at some of the issues the board and director of comms will need to watch.

Firstly, what do we mean by stakeholders? It has replaced the term 'publics' and 'audiences' that some of us used in our training. Literally it means people who have a stake in what our organisation is doing. In practice, people usually use the term to refer to organisations and people who are connected with us in some way – either because they are affected by what we do, or because they have a view on what we do. Although, technically, it can be all-encompassing and include the media, people don't usually list the media as a stakeholder – though it is a very important channel to them.

As chief executive it is likely that you will be meeting the most important stakeholders. How do you prioritise your time, and, most importantly, how do you ensure that your engagement benefits the comms effort?

And for CE and comms director, one of the toughest realities is that you don't have a handle on all the stakeholder engagement that is happening all over your organisation. The operations team are meeting the customers and industry groups, the strategy team are meeting the Government, the field team are meeting the public and so on and so on. When you are launching a new initiative, or involved in something controversial, or when a stakeholder falls out with you – then you are involved. The rest of the time it's all just happening.

The benefits of this are that the stakeholders have a relationship with the most relevant people in your organisation. They are part of day-to-day business with your organisation. They feel they have a personal contact instead of just being funnelled through an enquiry desk. This is very valuable.

The problem is that you can look incompetent with stakeholders if the person meeting with them doesn't know about a key piece of information, ("But you announced yesterday that you are shutting the Crewe office, didn't you know?"). Or if the stakeholder is visited by different people from your organisation in the same week without your internal colleagues knowing ("Nice to see you, we saw Bob from your place only yesterday, you could have come together…")

Can you and should you do anything about this? Well, yes and no.

Yes, you can map who is meeting who and you can decide – probably with other colleagues on your director team – whether these are the right people. Are they trustworthy? Do they have the right information?

Yes, you can take a keen interest in what stakeholders are saying to you. It's a good idea to have an item on your regular directors' team meetings reviewing what external stakeholders are saying. In my experience, senior people usually have these meetings and then keep the information to themselves. Not because they are being selfish, just because they are busy and don't appreciate the importance of letting everyone else know.

When you have worked out (through stakeholder mapping) who the really powerful stakeholders are, you should then ensure that any engagement with them, and lessons learned, are shared with your senior colleagues. Your colleagues will be meeting this same stakeholder, perhaps at more junior or regional levels of their organisation, and the messaging and myth-busting needs to be consistent right the way through if you are going to have the influence you need.

I used to make specific note of when my director colleagues were meeting key stakeholders and talk to them about it. Sometimes before – to see if they needed any information – but mostly afterwards, just for a chat to see how the land is lying.

If you work somewhere where the comms person is just seen as the person who does the media, the website and the staff newsletter you  might have to work harder at getting into this circle of information. But you need to – otherwise your advice isn't impacting where the real action is.

On the 'no' side, you probably won't be able to set up a sophisticated stakeholder management system where every meeting is listed on a database and every person who meets stakeholders can see what everyone else has said at previous meetings. There are products such as Asana, Trello and Wrike that help you do this, but they are only as good as the people putting the information in, and this is where they often fall down. If you are working at a place where you have a process that works – congratulations. It's more likely that – like me - you have tried, and found that people just don't let the comms team know what's happening, or get irritated when you chase them for a meeting note, or let you know about lots of minor meetings but nothing important because that can't be shared on an open database.

The theory suggests you should have this database, and if you have an organised person in your team who can run it it's not that difficult. In my experience it falls down because the senior people who meet the most senior stakeholders – and phone them, and exchange emails with them – are not going to spend time giving you feedback.

So, my suggestion is that you make this more informal. Drop by their office for a catch-up, have the item on the directors' agenda, have a weekly external affairs meeting to discuss it.

It's possible that you are a comms director reading this and thinking, "If only I had that problem! If only my senior team did meet stakeholders." One of the most important pieces of advice for stakeholder relations is that the first contact you make with them shouldn't be the one where you give them the bad news. "Hi, you don't know me, but I am the chief executive of ABC and we are going to bulldoze down your school."

Important relationships need to be built over time. This means that your senior team need to be engaged with your local MPs, or pressure groups, or regulators, or media on a regular basis. It doesn't have to be frequent – they probably haven't got time. But it does have to be enough time to build some trust: for you to understand their issues, and for them to understand yours. It will help your senior team gain an insight into what matters to your stakeholders and vice-versa. If you do need to do something controversial, at least you will have had time to share the reasons for it in a calm manner, over time.

In the strategy and planning section, I stress the importance of knowing which stakeholders really can make a difference, the ones that really have the power. Make sure you build a relationship over time with these people. They probably won't be knocking at your door. They could be hidden within an organisation and difficult to get to. A planning official, a procurement director, a policy lead, the chair of a key committee.

If you can't get to meet them, try at least to meet the people that might influence them. Their researcher for example. Don't give up just because they aren't knocking on your door.

At CSCI, we didn't leave the stakeholder relations just to when we were launching something new like star ratings, we had regular stakeholder drinks evenings. These were at our offices in central London, towards the end of the working day. The chair, chief inspector and other board members were there. There would perhaps be a short speech on something new or current but mostly time to mingle. The stakeholders wanted to meet each other as much as us, so they worked very well.

## Co-design

In public services at the moment co-design is a buzz word. It means that you will have a better plan, and your stakeholders will have more commitment to a plan, if they have been part of its creation.

It's a very good aim to have, but it requires some work. And – obviously – it needs to happen before the key decisions are made. Or at least at a time when they can be shaped. These sorts of consultations often fail – and harm your reputation – because people think (sometimes correctly!) that the decision has already been made and consultation is therefore superficial and meaningless.

If you work at an organisation that places a high emphasis on the importance of involving your customers and users in decisions, you will need a well-planned and comprehensive approach to making sure they have the channels to have their say. You, also, will want to make sure that the evidence you get from this work is accurate. For example, if you have one 'user' on your board you will get that one person's view – and perhaps those of their friends. That doesn't equate to "what customers want/need". And it's a really difficult position to put someone in. It doesn't mean that you shouldn't have that person on the board, it means you need a broader approach, too.

You won't be able to find solutions that everyone is happy with. So, you will need to design a process that most people are happy with for reaching the decision.

At an NHS primary care trust where I worked, they were consulting with patients and other stakeholders about changes to maternity services. They agreed – with patient involvement – a set of success criteria that would be used to judge the different options. These included how safe the option would be for mothers and babies, which was given extra weighting.  After all the consultation work the options each had their final score.  Anyone who wanted to campaign for an option that had a lower score, was therefore going against the scoring that the patients and other stakeholders themselves had set.  This independently verified scoring system was very powerful in helping the community and the NHS reach – and accept – the right decision.

I worked with CSCI (the social care regulator) from its inception.  The Board had set a very high expectation of the involvement of people using social care services in the decision making of the regulator.  There was  a dedicated team to manage this and several standing groups who reported into the organisation.   I chaired the diversity group – people with disabilities representing the interests of people with diverse age profiles, ethnicity and sexuality. The fact that was a standing group meant that we didn't have to randomly pull people together to ask them something. They knew they had a regular place where they could raise issues, and so did we.

## Conclusion

Stakeholder relations is the powerhouse of your comms. Media relations may have the greater effect on reputation – and the greater call on your time, but stakeholder relations has more effect on your organisation's effectiveness. Try to make sure that when you are discussing comms as a senior team your conversations are as much about stakeholder issues as they are about media.

Chapter Five

# Branding, Public Affairs, Campaigns

It was my first visit to the impressive Lord's ground in north London, but I wasn't there to play cricket. I was speaking at a conference. The witty compere decided to get a few laughs as he introduced me by holding up a card a metre wide which he said was my business card because my job title was so long. And it was. Director of Communications, User and Public Involvement.

The tasks we have covered so far usually form the core of the role, but there are usually a lot more disciplines related to the communications field that you will be responsible for. As I mention in the introduction, I won't cover everything. However, the three disciplines of branding, public affairs and campaigns are so closely aligned with comms that I think they need their own sections.

# Branding

- **How do you ensure that your brand is supporting your organisation goals?**
- **'The brand is more than the logo' – is this true in practice?**
- **How can you steer a branding project through a tricky board meeting?**

At my prestigious golf club, the new brand was launched to the members. Not a revolution, but an evolution to fit the modern culture so that we could move our club on from our slightly old-fashioned image. Complaints flooded back into the staff office based on all sorts of personal preferences, myths and gossip. The management decided to have a referendum. I was seething quietly that a properly thought-out change to fit our business objectives was going to become decided by hundreds of people with no knowledge at all of branding.

And therein lies the problem for every branding project that I have ever worked on. The design element of branding – a bunch of colours, shapes and letters – is easy for everyone to judge, whether they know about branding or not. And, unfortunately for the branding experts, some of those people are in the decision-making chain.

I have sat round so many board room tables where the design company present the suggested new brand identity and the board members say, "but it looks like a kite", or "I don't really like that shade of red: it doesn't go with anything." I think branding consultants have the patience of saints.

You cannot afford to get this wrong, though. The brand is the character and personality of your organisation, so it needs to be aligned with your business goals. It also takes years to embed itself in the minds of your publics so don't change it lightly, but if you do, do it on the basis of evidence combined with good intuition.

Here are a few tips from my experience.

### *Follow the business plan, not just your favourite colour*

Make sure that the branding and brand values are based on the explicit mission and strategic plan of the organisation, not on someone's preferences. The brand is just one part of the delivery of your goals so it must align.

And, if possible, ensure that the brand of your organisation extends right through everything your organisation does. At CSCI the board were clear from the outset that it would be listening to and championing people using social care services. This belief and commitment ran through the organisation like the word Brighton through a stick of rock. The logo was a speech bubble and handwriting, to indicate dialogue.

However, when I did the NHS rebranding project in 1999 the sheer scale, complexity and diversity of the NHS meant that there was no way we could achieve such a goal. Instead we took the overriding goal of the White Paper at the time "One NHS" and made sure that this drove our visual branding policy.

Even if you don't have a handle on staff behaviours and culture, you do have a handle on tone of voice and style of pictures. When I was director of advocacy and comms at Christian Aid, we never used a photo of a person that robbed them of their dignity. Other charities may use pictures of people suffering with flies in their eyes, but Christian Aid doesn't.

## Research base

If you are leading a branding project one vital foundation is independent research. Budget properly for this so that your decision makers are able to see how the current brand is performing with your target audiences and then the kind of attributes they would like to see in an organisation like yours. This helps when you get to the decision-making stage and someone is speaking from personal preference rather than evidence.

## Specialist advice and gut feel

I think that in a large or medium-sized organisation using a specialist branding agency is vital – not just a lone designer or your in-house team. There is so much more to a brand than design, and there is so much more to getting a branding project through an organisation than turning up at the top meetings with a very large folder containing nice words and pictures. A specialist consultancy can really help you to navigate your way through the process, and all the myriad individual preferences and ideas that arise during the development phases.

And the flip-side of that coin is – don't just rely on the specialist consultancy. You are the person that knows your organisation inside out. If you are the comms director, you will have a gut feel and intuition about what is right for the character and aspirations of your business. Be open-minded but use your gut feel up against the other evidence. I remember many years ago the government department in charge of jobs and benefits being advised by a big agency to rename their job centres to the single, meaningless word 'One', following the trend set by 'Next' and 'Virgin'. The wise (and new) comms director thankfully over-ruled.

### Is rebranding the answer?

Don't be too quick to rebrand. There is a reason that we easily recognise and trust Heinz beans, Coca-Cola, the NHS and the BBC – their brands have evolved rather than metamorphosed. Rebranding isn't a magic solution if your reputation is fading or you are not cutting through. Make sure that you also look at whether your marketing spend and strategy is sufficient, or whether your customer service or products are actually what is affecting your brand. Rebranding projects can have a bad reputation in themselves so if you are doing one, know what you are getting yourselves in to. And if your research comes back saying that your visual identity isn't the problem – be brave enough to stick with what you have got. I have noticed often that staff within an organisation think a brand is 'tired' long before the public do. Having said that, sometimes bravery is making the change. Don't limp on with a brand that is telling the world you are one thing when you know you are another.

### Decision making – take people with you

Rebrand projects can be threatening to people so try to take people with you on the journey. A branding reference group, discussion workshops looking at character, audiences and market positioning plus lots of updates will help with this. It will also help to reinforce for people the real objectives you are trying to meet in rebranding, not just that the top team fancy a new logo.

### Set practical rules and follow them

There are many practical rules for a new visual identity. Does the logo shrink small for social media? Does the strapline work and does it sit neatly within the logo so that it doesn't just get cut off? Is the logo too easy to redraw badly? (If you are charity and your logo will be reproduced by hundreds of local volunteers try and make sure it isn't too simple so that people have to use the jpeg picture file.)  Does it work in single colour? Does it work for people with visual impairment?  Set the rules out clearly first so that everyone can check the options against them.  This is particularly useful when you are steering the identity through the board, who will intuitively use their own subjective judgment of the new identity if there are no other criteria set down to evaluate against.

### Ongoing brand management

These tips are about rebranding and brand refresh projects but on a day-to-day basis the comms department is probably just managing an existing brand. This isn't easy and the name 'brand police' gets used liberally by other teams.  I think it does make sense for the comms department to have overall ownership of brand issues, even if it gets them a lot of grief. Clear protocols and rules will help, and making sure that your brand team understand the business objectives of their colleagues so that they don't just appear as design police is helpful, too. When your brand is being reproduced locally by multiple local offices and teams then 'make it easy to get it right' is my best advice. Templates, advice and guidance are central to this.

# Public affairs

- **How can you influence Government policy that affects your business?**
- **How much of the  political relationship work should you do yourself?**
- **Are your early-warning systems for crucial legislation good enough?**

'Democracy is the worst form of Government except for all those other forms that have been tried,' quoted Churchill. What a true phrase.

Government policy and action is influenced by so many factors. Perhaps it's a story that has gripped the public mind and results in loud calls for government action such as a dangerous dog killing a child or a much-loved football club going bust. It might be the views of a celebrity or sports star such as footballer Raheem Sterling talking about racism or Jeremy Clarkson's rejection of climate change reduction policies. It can be populist manifesto pledges, for example Boris Johnson promising to bring back hop-on, hop-off buses in London during his campaign for Mayor.

It's sadly also true that some areas of government policy are heavily  influenced by very superficial public understanding of what is required to achieve change. When I was working on public policy the area of  crime and justice was most affected by this. The policies that the public want (more police on the streets, capital punishment, lock up youth offenders) aren't the policies that will actually reduce crime.

And, of course, all government policy has to take into account the essentially self-interested nature of all of us. People don't want to give up smoking, drinking, playing violent computer games, drive gas-guzzling cars etc etc. Governments that ask them to don't get broad support.

In addition, politically driven media coverage can have a huge impact. The undermining of the MMR vaccinations in 1998 started with the later-discredited view that it's linked with autism, but the story was driven along much harder because the right-wing press wanted to push the Labour Prime Minister, Tony Blair, on whether his children had been vaccinated, while he was trying to say his children's health issues were private. The flaky claims, based on only 12 cases, resulted in many, many people not using the vaccination and the return of measles.

What this all adds up to is that Governments and politicians are rarely given the spaces to develop evidence-based, well-thought-out policies. And the relevance of this for this book is that this can have an effect on your business, and you might want to do something about it.

Planned and effective public affairs is not only desirable, but essential. If you and your organisation have views and information that can support positive political activity and legislation, you owe it to yourselves (and wider society) to make sure that it is shared in the right places.

There are two elements you need in place. Firstly, the relationship that the senior people in your organisation have with the relevant government departments, or local government people, that cover your work. Secondly, the arrangements that you have in place for knowing what is happening with legislation and debates that affect your work.

The latter will usually be done by your public affairs manager who may also be the person who keeps in touch with the relevant researchers, committees, special advisers etc.

Your public affairs activity will benefit from having a good process for knowing what is happening both at a publicly-shared level (dates for debates, questions in the House etc) and at the level of developing thinking that hasn't been shared publicly (trends, private conversations, who is lobbying who). For the latter your public affairs team need to have working relationships with the right people. I have been fortunate to work with several very good public affairs managers and the quality of their 'little black book' is usually very impressive (as is their knowledge of the pubs of Whitehall).

Depending on your own background, you may have contacts and relationships in government that are useful to your organisation – a quick look at your diary will show whether your time is being spent on the most influential people. Don't neglect your useful contacts because you get so busy with other things. And if you don't have them, try to build them. As a directors team it is important that you are in positions where you can influence. Multiply the number of routes into the government department by making sure you are connected to your professional equivalent. So, for example, the director of comms or the director of HR. What can you offer them either as advice or information or through your public affairs team?

As for the key relationships that your other senior colleagues need to maintain, these are likely to be the bread and butter of their work. If not, you may need to encourage them to take these relationships seriously, and especially to build a relationship over time so that you have some depth of relationship for when you need to be persuasive over an unpopular political trend or decision.     Having worked at Number 10 and other government departments I know how influential and useful these conversations can be to politicians and their staff so don't neglect them.

As director, what are you looking for in your public affairs team?  You will want the basics in place: a well-informed diary and early-warning system for government action and political activity that affects you.  Then you will want to be assured that the team are making the connections with the right people – the right researchers, or civil servants, that will give you both the soft information that you need and the routes to provide information of your own.  While we often recruit public affairs managers because of their ability to network and their knowledge of the political system, don't neglect the importance of skills in analysis of information (this might be shared with more policy-minded people) and project management – for example making sure that you get your responses to government consultations in on time, tied to a comms plan with stakeholders and staff if necessary.

Also, we need to remember that the impact of good public affairs work can take a long time to be realised. Trusted relationships take a long-time to develop so it could be several years before your organisation is able to contribute information to a key piece of legislation.  Play the long game.

Finally, be helpful to everyone you meet in politics - they move around so often. Helping that annoying researcher who pestered you for information when they were at the Home Office could benefit you hugely when they are appointed as special adviser in the Treasury.

# Campaigns

- **How do you choose your campaign when the choice of subjects is so big?**
- **How do you run campaigns that genuinely make a difference?**
- **What are the pitfalls in running campaigns?**

The biggest risk with campaigns is that you get drawn into running too many, for too little time and then they keep everyone very busy but have very little effect.

In the public sector, campaigns are usually about awareness or behaviour change (register to vote; stop smoking; renew your driving licence). In charities 'campaigning' usually refers to efforts to change the behaviour of particular groups of people (often businesses) or government policy (boycott Starbucks, reduce plastic use, save tigers). In commercial organisations they will be sales and marketing campaigns and the public relations and media plans that support them (20% off this month only; launching the new XR range.)

As communications director you have to make sure that the campaign fits the strategic priorities and that it is sufficiently robust to have some effect. Campaigns that essentially just entertain the supporters, or the comms team, or a policy team, are a waste of money unless you have specifically set that as an objective.

I am sceptical about charity campaigns for legislation change or business change that are essentially to build your profile or make the supporters feel engaged. Those can be added benefits, but probably a sad waste of effort that undermines other more serious campaigning attempts. My experience of talking to businesses who are the targets of campaigning activity is that they often incorrectly think the only purpose of campaigns is for the charity to raise money. That's not only not true, but some of the campaigns I have been involved in, such as the early campaigns to reduce climate change, were actually bad for public fundraising because public sentiment had not moved far enough at that stage.

If you are running short campaigns, or lots of campaigns, ask yourself or your team whether they will have the impact desired. Campaigns need to be targeted, research-based, highly-planned but also flexible enough to react to events, and last long enough to have a chance of breaking into the minds of the target audiences and shifting attitudes and behaviour.

As chief executive or another director, think twice about requesting or allowing these short campaigns unless you have good evidence that they can be effective. That doesn't mean that your campaign shouldn't use short 'bursts' – these can be a very good way to maximise attention at one time. It means that it shouldn't just be one short burst, and then move on to another subject.

Most comms teams will have experience of multiple demands from senior people, supporters and work colleagues to run different campaigns. It helps if you have an agreed process in your organisation for how campaigns are agreed including criteria that they must meet. Then it can't just be a case of someone trying to persuade the comms director.

Make sure, too, that the campaign is part of an overall mission by your organisation to change behaviour on a subject – not just a comms exercise. The public sector are sometimes guilty of trying to use limited advertising campaigns to change public behaviour when it would be more effective to just change the way the public service works to fit the way people want to use it. The NHS have been trying for many years to persuade the public not to turn up at A&E for minor illnesses. Some areas of the country have accepted that it's easier just to put a GP surgery in A&E than it is to change public behaviour.

The senior influence that you need to have on the campaign is to ensure that it is research-based and evaluated, and to ensure that it is given the time it needs to work. Changing opinion and behaviour will, in most cases, need to be a long-term project, often over many years, and campaigns mustn't be changed on a whim or on flaky evidence.

You will also probably need to limit the number of other campaigns that are run from the same organisation to the same target audiences. It will be the job of the senior team to prioritise and to be tough about stopping, or rejecting, small or adhoc campaigns that might limit the exposure for your primary campaigns. .

Another crucial issues for the directors is to ensure that your own organisation is following the demands given in your campaigns. This isn't easy but you need to at least be aware of it. The Church of England finding that its own investors were supporting loan-sharks when the Archbishop of Canterbury launched his campaign against them is a good example. The Department of Health can't ensure that all its staff give up smoking and use the stairs not the lift, but they can ensure that there are schemes in place to help people. And with your organisation policies, remember that your organisational narrative needs to include your campaign messages, or at least not undermine them.

## Conclusion

The comms director's job will often cover many smaller disciplines and you may not be the expert on all of them. As a general rule, for each area you can ask:

- Does this support and help meet our organisational goals (or is it just someone's 'good idea')?

- Is what we are doing based on research and evidence?

- Are we giving enough time and resources to this to make it worthwhile and have an impact?

## Chapter Six

# Research and Evaluation

- **Why do comms departments undervalue evidence?**
- **When is research money wasted and when is it essential?**
- **What are the risks in setting performance measures for comms?**

It was the Monday morning meeting in the Government department where I was working. I was sitting around the table with the Minister's special adviser and the strategy team and we were talking about what government policy should be on a particular issue. The special adviser mentioned that he had had lunch with friends the day before and they had some very interesting views on what the most difficult issues were and how to solve them.

Thankfully, before this research group of two became the evidence for millions of pounds of government spend, the thoughts and ideas were put into proper research (usually, but wrongly, called 'polling' in politics).

But how often is that not the truth? How often does someone say to you 'I was talking to a friend who said that we should launch our own app' and then expect that it will happen?

Big decisions should be based on evidence and analysis. This is essential for most areas of work, and absolutely essential in reputation and stakeholder management where people are tempted to think they know what others' think based on just their own networks and perceptions.

In the charity world fundraisers know there are some people who will never donate much to anything. Their arguments might be 'it all gets spent on admin' etc. Their views will be loud and strong, but they are not worth much of the charity's attention. The people the charity needs to fully understand are those that can be moved from 'interested but not active' into 'active'. I have worked with some great professional fundraisers. They are excellent at segmenting their audiences based on research and then designing their plans around the results.

Comms departments have a patchy reputation for using research formally, often because of the reactive nature of much of our work. Yes, we have instinctive knowledge of what our target audiences read, and what the most popular channels are, but this may not be enough as a foundation for an important comms project. Commissioning bespoke research or checking existing research can be really useful if done well.

The strategic decision comms directors need to make is when and when not to spend money on research. It can be the spark that ignites your strategy, or it can be an expensive way of being told what you could have found out from a quick chat by the water cooler with your team or a few hours of easy desk research.

For example, you can buy into big sector-wide research to show how your unprompted awareness score has shifted from one year to the next. Perhaps, you learn that you have moved from 12% one year to 13% the next. Is that useful? Is it even within the margin of error for the statistics? It's useful around the board table because it is useful for decision-makers to see how we sit relative to competitors, and it can underline the value of comms spending. But has that money really told you something you needed to know? Had you changed your practice so showing a small positive trend? Or has it told you very little at all?

Or you can do some niche stakeholder research that reveals that key people didn't know about your expertise in a mission-critical area, and if they did, your reputation would be much stronger. There's your gap and that piece of research is worth the spend.

Thankfully, the emphasis on good evaluation for comms has increased healthily over the years and the Chartered Institute of Public Relations training and advice is well-worth using.

I think the three most important purposes for your research are, firstly, to inform your strategy and plan in the first place – to make sure that you are not making incorrect assumptions about what stakeholders think and to segment audiences so that you can target them effectively. Then to test any specific actions or treatments that you might use (messaging, visuals, approaches). And finally, and the most difficult, to aid evaluation – to measure how successful your interventions have been so that you can shift the dial if necessary.

## Informing the plan

For the first purpose you can choose from the full suite of research methods: desk research, surveys, interviews, focus groups, deliberative events, omnibus surveys. Work with a good research company to get the brief really precise so they understand what it is you want to know and why. Although you probably need an indicative plan in order to get your competitive quotes, don't be afraid to then use their expertise to use the budget in different ways - perhaps you need more qualitative research (eg interviews or focus groups), or a variety of shorter quantitative surveys (eg a multiple choice online survey) to get to the core of what you need to know. It isn't unusual for you to get the research results back and then know what questions would have been much more helpful. Don't spend money asking things that you know already (unless you need this to persuade senior colleagues.)

## Testing your approach

For testing particular treatments, you will probably want to use qualitative methods, such as focus groups or other face-to-face techniques. And you will probably want to be present at some of these groups so you get a proper sense of people's reactions, which is sometimes more powerful than the report the agency give you afterwards.

A colleague says that observing the focus groups was a real eye-opener when he was working for the Liberal Democrat party. One example he recalls was reactions to the word 'radical'. It's much loved by politicians and policy makers but, in connection with different and impactful transport options, the focus group reaction saw 'radical' as code for cumbersome, expensive and daft.

Qualitative techniques are especially useful for discerning whether the approach hits the right emotional tone. How does it make people feel? This is less easy to grasp accurately through simple surveys.

## Measurement and evaluation

Research can be one of the tools you can use to set benchmarks that will be used to evaluate whether your comms plan is effective. However, remember that if you do use research, opinion shifts in audiences often move very slowly and by small percentage points. Don't get your hopes up too high.

You can also evaluate using quantifiable behaviour measures, for example: an increase in calls to the helpline; a reduction in social media posts about a sticky myth; an increase in sales.

An undervalued evaluation method in my opinion is the views of peers. This is not useful for a numbers-based dashboard but can be a useful steer for the project leaders. It just means asking some well-chosen people how they think the campaign has gone, what has worked well and what hasn't. It can be more useful than trying to find a measure.

If you are devising evaluation measures mostly to fit the organisation's business monitoring processes, then there are several factors to take into account.

Be aware that it is challenging to set measurement targets for comms work because of the often-unquantifiable nature of what we do. Shifting opinions and thought leadership aren't easily counted for a monthly report. Most organisations have a numbers-driven dashboard though so making wise choices of a few key measures is very important to prove to the board your effectiveness and to ensure that your team get proper recognition for their achievements.

You will need to use other methods to demonstrate effectiveness for work that isn't measurable – correcting bad media stories being the obvious one.

Be very careful that you don't get pushed into agreeing

to measures that will have a perverse effect on your team's work. Many organisations have a performance department producing dashboards and project plan analyses to check that the organisation is on track with meeting the business objectives. I have found it difficult to work with these teams to get the right measures for comms.

At the Commission for Social Care Inspection there was discussion about setting the engagement team a target of numbers of people attending events. However, we argued against this because the value of our engagement was in what we found out, and in reaching some seldom-heard groups. If we got green rated just for attracting high numbers we would have designed very different events.

You will also need to judge the culture of the organisation to know how important quantifiable measures are. The most illuminating methods can be expensive. The clearest example of this is with media relations. My first job in PR was with General Accident Property Services – a national estate agents. My MD, a salesman by background, asked me to set my targets for getting our name in the papers in our region. I gave him a column inches target, he added 25% to that number and that was what he then judged me on. Not very scientific but it did the job. Column inches (yes, inches) were very popular a few decades ago.

Then the industry came up with the idea of 'AVE' (advertising value equivalent) to create some huge numbers with pounds signs on to impress everyone. These are unpopular nowadays though. A much simpler 'mentions' and perhaps 'reach' score suffices if you need something straightforward. You can spend big money on in depth analysis from a specialist media evaluation company and be given a wealth of detail. To get the most out of this you need really think about what you want to know, and why. Will the information be used, and will it inform your practice? If yes, or occasionally to set a strategy, then go ahead. If not, you might be better to spend your money on another press officer.

## Conclusion

There are two risks with research: not doing any, guessing what people think and then essentially wasting money on badly targeted comms. Or, spending too much and finding out things that either aren't really useful, or that you know anyway. Be strategic in how you spend your money. And for monitoring dashboards make sure you have well-chosen quantifiable evaluation measures so that your work is recognised, but don't fall into the trap of choosing a bad target if the area of work can't really be measured in that way.

Chapter Seven

# Crisis Management

- **How do you plan in advance for unexpected events?**
- **Why is good comms is at the heart of a good response?**
- **How can you protect your reputation when the worst happens?**

I was working for a development charity and the phone rang one Christmas Eve. Armed soldiers had stormed one of our offices in Africa, shooting a guard and clearing out the office for immediate closure. As I engaged in the ensuing teleconferences a small part of my brain thought longingly about the half-finished glass of wine downstairs while the rest of me accepted that this was a life and death issue and my Christmas comfort was way down the list of priorities.

The awful fire at Grenfell Tower; the disappearance of Malaysian Airlines flight 370; 'mad cow' disease hits beef stocks; Gerald Ratner calling his products 'crap'; risk of salmonella in some Galaxy chocolate bars; the Marchioness pleasure boat crash; the Croydon tram crash; patient kills nurse.

Awful things happen. As a directors' team you will probably at some point face a tragedy, mistake or crisis that means you need to drop everything and respond.

As communications director you should be at the heart of the response team from the beginning. Well-managed comms can reduce the fear and suffering for people involved, help with the rescue or mitigation efforts and, of course, protect your valuable reputation so that you can continue to operate.

Your initial response will hopefully be dictated by your crisis response plan. It isn't difficult to think in advance what could go wrong. It is a lot more difficult to make this job come to the top of anyone's to-do list and write up the necessary plan. It's sometimes worth asking a PR student on work placement, or someone who has just finished another project, to put together the pack that contains everyone's contact numbers, plus a first draft of how you might react to various predictable disasters. (If you at least have a draft it's easier to get people to engage with it.) This can include Q&As and the background information mentioned below. It should give you some ideas for initial statements that can be used on social media at the beginning.

The other useful result of brainstorming what could go wrong is that you can put in place mitigating actions to stop it happening. Reputational risk should be on your organisational risk register for this reason.

The first thing you will need is as much information as you can find about what has happened. When a crisis occurs, social media will probably be full of it. Talk to your staff, get someone looking at what's online. Find out the facts, you will need them, because your reaction will need to be fast.

There will be multiple aspects to your organisations' response, and some of these the comms director will want to ensure are covered and in place.

When I was training comms people on how to do this, I invented an acronym as a sort of checklist for whether your response for the public and stakeholders is covering the right bases.

CRISES:   Context, Reassurance, Information, Support, Empathy, Stakeholders.

**Context** – sometimes, but not always, your responses and statements can reduce panic by giving some context to how often these things happen, how likely they are, how damaging they are, etc.  "This is the first time this has happened in ten years of operations".  "We are very sorry for the disruption but would add that we have the lowest number of breakdowns in Europe."

**Reassurance** – what are you telling people you are going to do to stop this happening again?  Will it happen again?  What safety procedures are in place?  Are you doing an investigation? What's your safety record?  Do people need to worry?  What should they do if they are worried?

**Information** – there are two aspects to this.  Firstly, make sure you give all the information that people will want to know – phone numbers, background, names, details.  Be as thorough as you can.  Secondly, the media will be told to fill acres of space if there is a disaster – if you don't give them information to fill this space, they will find it from the internet and other commentators.  Therefore, make available as much background information as you can. What type of train was it? Do you have a plan of the train? How long have you been running these types of trains?

**Support** – helplines, counsellors, stewards – whatever type of support your crisis needs, make sure it is available fast. Make sure that your usual routes for phone calls – the customer service centre or your front-line offices – know what to say to people.  You will need to do this almost before you actually know what the support processes are because the phone calls won't wait.

**Empathy** – your actions, tone of voice and expressed understanding of the awful impact on the people involved is crucial. Your organisation may have gone into practical responses mode, or even back-covering mode, but your actions, statements and interviews must show your compassion. To make a connection with the audiences they need to see that your organisation, and your spokespeople, are human, too. This doesn't necessarily mean that you have to concede fault if that's not clear. It's OK to say 'if we have done something wrong, we will put it right...' What is sometimes missed here is that the media, social media and staff will watch how your senior team react. Did they come back from holiday? Are they still taking their bonus? Did they visit the scene and talk to their own staff?

**Stakeholders** – in the midst of the immediate demands don't forget to think broadly about who needs to receive information. It is easy to fall into the trap of thinking about the big stakeholders – media and customers. However, there will be other people who will need to know. Suppliers, other stakeholders, interest groups, your own board members. If you have done the advance planning that's necessary, these distribution lists should be easily to hand. This will include making sure that the usual routes into your organisation – the call centre, local offices etc, have been given the necessary questions and answers.

You will need to make fast decisions about all of these things, and that is why planning in advance is so useful. In the immediate aftermath you will probably need a press office 'spokesperson' to hold the fort until you are able to make a more detailed statement and accept interview requests. Don't put your chief executive up for interviews until you have decided the immediate aspects of your response – even if that is to find out more. But don't delay too long or you may appear heartless and lacking in grip.

Finally, remember that the directors' meetings, or crisis response meetings, will be a bit high-energy. As comms director you will need to hold your own against everyone else who is – perhaps – panicking and trying to make sure their agenda is covered. In my experience the most difficult colleagues to deal with at this time are the legal team because our agendas are often directly opposing. If the organisation has done something wrong, should you say sorry? You might think that to rescue your reputation at all you need to say sorry fully and quickly. The legal team would probably disagree with you and claim that admitting liability could cost you thousands of pounds. The chief executive will need to make the final decision and what they probably need from the comms director is reasoning based on evidence, experience and logic rather than just gut feel and passion.

## CRISES in action: the rollercoaster

How could this look in practice? In June 2015 an accident on the Smiler rollercoaster ride at Alton Towers caused devastating injuries to passengers. The accident was avoidable.

Afterwards, owners Merlin Entertainments were widely considered to have handled the response to the accident well, with the chief executive appearing quickly on media interviews, taking full responsibility and expressing sympathy for the victims.

Just looking at the online response now, we can see how the company fulfils the CRISES checklist.

**Context** – early interviews with the chief exec emphasise safety aspects of rollercoasters, particularly when challenged about previous problems with the ride stopping. "When you are on a rollercoaster car it can't come off the track and you are strapped in." Contextual numbers aren't given for this accident but in an online commentary of the accident a US trade body says: "The likelihood of being seriously injured (require overnight hospitalisation for treatment) on a permanently located amusement park ride in the US is 1 in 24 million." If figures are appropriate these are the kind of statistics that are useful.

**Reassurance** – safety is a main theme of their response. The park was closed immediately for an investigation; the statements referred to safety processes. A few days later when returning visitors were interviewed by the media this comment was typical: "We arrived fairly early and we could see all the test ones going round. What will they have been doing for the past few days? You know that they will have just been checking everything, so the rides that are going today are probably the safest they've been in a very long time."

**Information** – the early media reports are full of facts and figures about the ride (and, understandably, a list of other safety breaches). Also, Merlin quickly let customers with tickets know that they could have a full refund or change their date because the park was closed.

**Support** – a helpline number is given. A senior staff member of Merlin hand-delivers a letter to each victim. Compensation is promised.

**Empathy** – From the beginning the statements express sympathy for the victims and give priority to their suffering. 'Our heart goes out to them' says the chief executive. The hand-delivered letters are a symbol of this in action.

**Stakeholders** – The customer comments are encouraging. And one media channel interviews someone who runs a fan group for Rollercoasters, who says: "For an accident like this to happen does surprise me because they are a reputable company and they have got a lot of technology to prevent this happening."

## Conclusion
Don't forget that most crises can be planned for – not just thinking up all the awful things that could happen but keeping an eye on trends in public opinion. For example, ten years ago using plastic straws would not have caused any ripples. Today, if a campaign group named your organisation as the most prolific users of plastic straws you will be under siege. So, lesson one is plan in advance. Lesson two is get your message out there before others and make it human. Think and respond with your heart and not just your brain or your wallet and you may be able to ease people's suffering and maintain your good reputation.

# Part Two:
# Director of Communications –
# the Job in Practice

## Chapter Eight

# Know Yourself

Early in my career, I spent a ghastly weekend thinking that I was going to be sacked on Monday for incompetence. I was in charge of publishing a printed newsletter from the regional office. It was full of important facts and figures. Earlier in the week I squirmed as I had to tell the boss that the whole print run had to be done again because of a mistake in the figures. We had the changes made, I proofread the changes, I ordered the new print. Phew. Then the new print run arrived and to my horror, I noticed that the changes had affected another section that I hadn't checked. Could I tell the boss, again, that we needed to do a third print run? How could I be so incompetent?

The answer, I later found out when I did personality profiling, is because I am not naturally a detail person. A detail person would have checked not only the new changes, but any knock-on effects. It's not an excuse, it's a reason for me to be very mindful of my strengths and weaknesses when I am in a situation where something I am weak at is very important. Detail makes me feel stressed, uncomfortable and apathetic. But, because I know this now, I know that I have to steel myself and find strategies to ensure that the detail is covered.

The most important progress that I have made in being a communications manager has come from understanding myself better. It matters for several reasons:

- In our role, gut feel about how people behave, their

opinions, their reactions, their preferences, is a key skill. We need to be able to separate out what is 'us' and what is others.

• The job of comms manager is almost entirely done through people. Managing our own team, managing the reputation of our organisation through the actions of others, managing our relationship with the Board. Understanding how different people tick is crucial for this, understanding how we tick is even more crucial.

I have done a variety of personality testing in various awaydays and training courses. The one that works for me is Myers Briggs – for those that understand these things I am an INFJ. I find myself thinking in these terms and assigning people to a type even when I don't know what their type is in order to help me work with them productively. (I have been teased by various chief executives for the annoying phrase "that's your J-ness coming out" and then being very careful with my phraseology if they are a P).

There are other types of personality profiling, choose the one that works best for you. A colleague prefers the simple shorthand of Sandy Cotter's Centaur model which summarises people as wizards, superheroes, good parents, poets or warriors. The title 'superhero' could have been invented for his boss alone, so faithful is he to his type. Others I know really value the quick shorthand of colour psychology, where people are rated as green, yellow, red or blue (or combinations: I am red-yellow).

In my experience, it's good to get professional help in assessing and understanding your type, not just a do-it-yourself test from the internet which I have known to be very inaccurate and misleading. This kind of profiling is frequently included in management courses and day-training and the professional will ensure that you truly understand what the profiling is telling you so that you can understand and adjust your behaviour accordingly.

Once you know yourself, the next logical task is to know your colleagues' types. In Myers-Briggs terms, lots of chief executives are ENTJ and ESTJs. Understanding how they tick will help you to work well with them.

An important caution that the books always give, though, is that you don't stick rigidly to the types and assume that everyone in a particular type is the same. Everyone has their own character, and this will be overlaid on their personality type. Yes, they will share some characteristics but the expression of them can be different. I have worked for lots of ENTJs and 'red' characters. Some I would love to work with again, some I will be very happy to never work with again.

Sexist language aside, I like the quote from Clyde Kluckhohn that Isabel Briggs Myers uses in her caution on this. "Every man is like every other man, every man is like some other men, every man is like no other man."

## Chapter Nine

# Managing Up and Across

- **How can you manage senior meetings when you are the only one who thinks like you do?**
- **How can you persuade your numbers-driven finance director?**
- **How do you manage your own emotional energy?**

As a director of communications you will have the joy of working with senior colleagues who have a wide range of different responsibilities and you will probably have a schedule of regular management meetings with them in your diary. These people are the bridge or the barrier to what you need to achieve. These relationships and meetings must not be undervalued.

### Working with the boss and senior people

Say you are at the level where your boss is the Chief Executive or another director. You could be working extensively with people who are dissimilar from yourself and have different day-to-day priorities. Comms directors are often the most outward-looking people on the directors' team and may be the bridge between the internal and external world. Here are some ways to make the relationships with your colleagues work efficiently.

### 1. Prioritise and priorities

The common phrase, "your top priority should be what's keeping your chief exec awake at night" is a good one for comms directors. Her priorities should be your priorities. You will lose credibility if you only think about the standard comms diary and pester her about the annual report sign off when she is worried about a dangerous security crisis.

Chief executives and senior people will expect you to understand the broader perspective in which they are working. If you are presenting them with an issue, make sure that your argument is mindful of the wider issues of the organisation. But also bring into play the external context that you may have a much better feel for.

In practice, it is often your own team who don't see, or have access to, the bigger picture. For them, the publication of the annual report is keeping them awake at night and they will be pestering you for the chief executive's sign off. You will find yourself having to find the right compromise position – explaining back to your team member the situation and having a conversation with the chief executive that makes sure she knows that the annual report does need to be done sometime.

### 2. Understand yourself and others

The previous chapter talks about the value of understanding personalities and it's a key skill for managing up.

At one organisation where I was director, the meeting between my team and the Chair was a weekly bloodbath. He would rant and rave, we would metaphorically cower in the corner and wonder where the next brickbat was coming from. Understanding his personality type helped to find the solution. The key facts from the personality profile stick in my mind, "ENTJs are natural critics. They set their own standards and are forceful in applying them to others…they abhor inefficiency or ignorance." We designed a detailed and ordered process to control and check everything that came to the meeting. This process involved his staff team. Instead of a weekly meeting where everything was up for discussion, which gave the impression that we hadn't done anything, we brought solutions that already had his team's buy in. ENTJs often want to see that an efficient machine is working to ensure that everything is correct and on time. If they can't see the machine or think that it only sparks up when they are watching, they get nervous. Our process was the machine, and it took the heat right out of the weekly meeting and meant everyone worked better.

Other personality types would hate this. They wouldn't want decisions closed down early and would want to be part of the discussion because they enjoy it. Understanding the boss is part of the solution.

Comms directors often find that they are misunderstood or undervalued around the boardroom table. This is often because they work intuitively. Other personality types need strong evidence, a rational argument, logic, science. The spooky gut feel of the comms director seems wishy-washy. I remember a wise chief executive in a conference speech telling comms managers "you have got to show them the working out on the side of the page." I have never forgotten that. You might know the right way forward - and you know it because you just know – finding the right way to explain that to the finance director is both a difficult challenge and a good discipline for us.

I am on the Strategic Delivery Committee of the board of the charity Mind. The External Affairs department are excellent at this. The papers we receive always have hard evidence and well-reasoned arguments to help the committee to make their comments and recommendations.

Understanding how people tick is one thing but also a fair amount of simple human empathy will also go a long way. For some chief executives and directors, the worst days of their year are when you tell them that they need to do a media interview or a conference speech. One of the best chief execs I worked for was brilliant with people but hated doing the media work. On a day full of media interviews, he was stressed and at a low ebb. He never shirked the responsibility – he just didn't enjoy it. Your support, and perhaps intervention to shift some interviews to a different spokesperson, might be crucial to keep your chief exec at his best.

Another chief exec relied on having his main messages written into a simple diagram. If that is what it took to enable him to be at his best, that is what we would do.

I have also frequently been surprised over the years to see how reluctant very competent bosses are to speak to the staff conference – or even at the staff Christmas party. One very confident, extroverted chief executive was quite happy to walk the floor, chat to the front-line, be the open and approachable chief exec but didn't place any value on doing a similar thing at his own senior managers conference – the people who really did need to hear from him.

There will also be times when your normally helpful colleagues become difficult to deal with. In these instances, you can often look behind the behaviour to see the fear, pressure or disappointment that are driving it. You might get the brunt of it, but it isn't about you really.

Being sensitive to the impact on people of what our job sometimes requires them to do means that we will, perhaps, spend extra time with them on preparation or make sure that other staff keep out of their way while their batteries are a bit drained.

### 3. Respect other disciplines

One of the great things about being a director is that you have access to senior colleagues with a really different set of skills. As with all teams, it's the total strength of the team that matters – not the brilliance of an individual. In sports parlance, a team with no world-class players can win if they are a good team, and a team full of world-class players can lose if they don't work as a team. The same is true of your director colleagues. Respecting them, benefitting from their wisdom and ensuring that they have access to your wisdom is very important. Respect them for what they offer and be available to help with their issues. Understand each other's priorities and you will go a long way towards finding shared team goals that work for the organisation.

My personal equivalent of the chief exec's dreaded day of media interviews was always the time of year when I had to do my annual budgeting. I joked with the finance director that I would be happier if she gave me my budget in 20 pages of lovely prose, than the standard set of spreadsheets. I would procrastinate tirelessly before I opened that file. She recognised my nervousness and gave me some of her time, and that of her senior staff, to help me meet my deadlines. I hope I repaid the favour when she needed a speech written.

### 4. The curse of the bright idea

I think there are some disciplines that suffer more from the tinkering of non-professionals than others.

Every time I work in branding, I witness that everyone has a view on whether the proposed new logo is too big, too bright, too cuddly, too trendy. I feel sorry for the designers who have to try and defend the logo against everyone's personal favourite style and colour.

The same is often true of comms. Everyone has a view on people issues, usually based on their own style. Few people would tell the Head of Legal what to do, however everyone has a view on how relationships and reputations should be managed. This presents a challenge for the comms director. We need to be wary of the person who is forthright in their view on how something should be expressed, or how a group should be treated, but isn't basing that on a wider analysis of what the particular audience think and believe, or the agreed strategy. We will need to find ways to contribute evidence, or an agreed process or an agreed strategy to the discussion to ensure a good decision is made.

I worked with a charity who had an excellent process for deciding what their priorities for campaigning would be. This subject is a minefield – passions are high when people are discussing which injustices should be tackled and which shouldn't. But they had a careful process that allowed for objective scoring. We then chose the subjects with the top scores and focussed efforts intensively on those subjects. This helped to deal with other people's very well-meaning and understandable 'bright ideas' for petitions that should be designed and letters to The Times written.

As you climb the career ladder you move further away from doing what you are told, towards championing what you believe is right. However, it's not always easy. You will need a very wise chief executive or chair in these situations. The best chair I worked with asked my opinion on proposed courses of action in the comms remit, listened to everyone's views on the risks and benefits, assessed all these with the evidence and then took a decision. You will find others who will dictate the approach largely based on how it would play with their peers or another inner circle.

One of your useful weapons in these instances is the

agreed comms strategy – which means agreed priorities. If you have this, you can argue that all projects have to fit into it and meet the standards you have set. If you are strong on evaluation, you can prove what works and what doesn't and show that your colleague's bright idea, though a useful contribution, hasn't worked in the past, or doesn't fit this audience group. This is adding some science and facts and figures to what you do to be persuasive.

How many comms people have been asked "we need a video/website/poster about X"? It's one of our standing jokes. Try and point people back to an agreed strategy. These are the messages we are concentrating on; we need to do it over a long period of time and we need to be consistent. If the video fits into this strategy it can be considered. If it can't it may be largely a worthless vanity project.

### 5. Falling out

I have been fortunate to work with very good chief executives and chairs from whom I have learnt a great deal. But even if this is true for you, things won't be perfect all of the time.

I recall a time when the chair was really not happy with me and it was the chief executive that was trying to tell me so. I asked if I could go and speak to the chair myself. The chief executive was lukewarm on this idea, but I wanted to have a go. I walked in to see the chair, we disagreed fairly strongly, I walked out with my bloodied nose and my orders. The chief exec asked me how I got on and I said, "I lost 5-1, but at least I got the one."

There will come a time when you will disagree with the boss. If you are unlucky you might work for a person you disagree with, or don't like, or don't respect, most of the time. And there will surely be a time when you don't work harmoniously with one of your director colleagues.

This generally hits comms people hard because our natural instinct is for good relationships with people. It's useful to know that it doesn't always hit other people so hard because they might not have this driver within their character. The poster "don't have a mud fight with a pig – you will get very dirty and they love it" was a very apt display in a colleague's office because of the nature of one of the top team that we had to work with.

Another lovely line in the Myer's Briggs book in the section on ENTJ's (the personality profile of a lot of chief executives) says: "some will even instigate issues when none exist just for the sake of having an argument."

So, prepare yourself for expending a lot of emotional energy if you are in this situation. It's not uncommon, so you need to know how to get through it but try not to let it define your whole working week. Make sure you keep going on the things that you are trying to do and are good at, rather than letting the disagreement, or difficult relationship, occupy your every waking thought.

There will always be a reason why this relationship is difficult. Try and get to the root of that and understand the situation from the other person's perspective. The "know yourself and know others" comments in chapter one are also key here. You will probably have to adapt your behaviour to fit their working style and preference. But equally, be true to yourself. Make sure that you can look at your own behaviour objectively and be proud of it. If you are not a person who shouts in meetings, don't start just because you are shouted at. If you are not usually a person who sends biting emails to a wide audience, don't start just because someone does it to you. Take a deep breath, let your anger subside, and decide rationally what the best way forward is.

Take advice from a mentor or senior colleague but try

not to dump too much of it on your own direct reports. It may feel cathartic at the time, but it will make them nervous and it can backfire if you need to push through a difficult decision from the Board and your team know that you are lukewarm about the people making the decisions.

I have had several spells in my senior career where a bad relationship has marred working life. It is really draining. I went on a resilience for women course when I was in the middle of one of these situations. One exercise that really worked for me was "imagine yourself in five years' time advising yourself now." Just vocalising that advice really helped me. It didn't cure the situation, but it helped me to survive. If you are in this situation, hang in there. You wouldn't have got to where you are now without having some skill, so have faith in your ability and work hard to resolve the issues or make the reasoned decision to move on.

One of the best pieces of advice I was given was "it will pass." When you are in it, it feels all consuming. However, you will look back on it in a year's time, or whenever, you will see that you did survive and probably learnt a lot from it.

## The Board and directors' team meetings

It was the first meeting that I had attended with the Prime Minister in the Cabinet room. On one side of the long table were the Home Secretary and his comms team, already seated. The Number 10 team filed into the room to sit at the other side of the table and wait for the PM. Trying to appear as though I did this every day of the week, I sat down in the next available seat. My kindly neighbour whispered to me, "That's the Prime Minister's chair". Not believing him immediately it then took me a further few seconds to stand up – with everyone watching – and move, by which time all the seats at the table were taken and I had to find a seat over by the back wall where I stayed silent, and probably red-faced, for the entire meeting.  It was indeed the Prime Minister's chair, which by tradition is always set at an angle so that they can get into it easily when they walk in after everyone else is seated.

Your first meeting chaired by The Boss can be a daunting experience.  But there are ways to make it easier.  Whether it's the board meeting, the executive team meeting, or your directorate senior team meeting, some basic principles can make it work effectively for you. Being effective at a directors' team meeting is about being prepared and managing your interventions.  Here are some tips.

## 1. Be prepared

*a. Prioritising your time* – You may not be able to read every word of every paper for every meeting – even though it does really help if you can.  So, at least make sure that you look at them enough to find out what the reputation and comms implications are.  Also, check the minutes to find out if you were expected to feedback on anything. Give yourself enough time to check with your team the latest state of play before you go into the meeting.

*b.  Checking issues with board members* – Another key skill for working with the board is how you work with individual non-executives (NEDs) or trustees outside the meetings. When I was at CSCI, one of the NEDs was particularly interested and experienced in ensuring the accessibility of comms for people with a  range of abilities and disabilities. He was generous with his time in allowing me to chat things through with him outside meetings so that he could give me constructive advice but also understand what we were trying to do. This had the advantage of making sure that he didn't have to take us to task in the meeting, but also meant I had a person around the table who could support us if the comments from the rest of the board took an unexpected or unwelcome turn.

NEDs and trustees don't usually want to create bad feeling by rubbishing your idea in the actual meeting. However, they will do it if they feel it's their only opportunity to comment and put something right. If you work in an environment where you are encouraged to work with the trustees or NEDs outside the meetings, then get the full benefit from this so that you and they are not put in a bad position.

This doesn't mean that you have to run every paper past them before you take it to a meeting. Save this for papers that you think could be misunderstood, or where you value the input of a third person who has some understanding of comms. It can be a lonely battle otherwise, and – in public meetings particularly – you won't be able to argue your corner as vehemently for fear of damaging the overall reputation of the organisation.

At Christian Aid, I highly valued the input of a trustee who had a lot of campaigning experience. I tried to ensure that he had all the information and context that he needed because I needed him to argue the corner for these issues so that it didn't just look like me banging my own drum.

Your chair and chief executive will need careful handling, too. Take great care to ensure they are not surprised by something major ('bounced'). Chief executives nearly always want to see papers before they go to the board, but it is also helpful for them if you let them know the contentious areas.

There are some rare exceptions to this – for example, if you trust the chair more on your issues than the chief executive – but generally a no surprises rule works best.

Prepare key issues in advance with your fellow directors, too. If you have read the papers and are worried about an issue, you don't have to wait for the meeting – you could ask them in advance. Hopefully they will do the same with you. The best senior teams that I have worked on had a respect for each other's expertise which meant that they would very rarely choose the senior team meeting or board meeting to criticise your paper. They would do this privately so that your working relationship is maintained.

### 2. Manage your interventions

This is the key skill for meetings: when and how to say what you want to say. Lots of items on the agenda will be very straightforward – a short discussion, an easy decision and move on. However, some won't be. There will be items that you are very concerned about. There will be items where you completely disagree with your colleagues. There will be discussions where you can feel the red rage building up from your chest to your face as it progresses. And there are items when the chair makes a decision that you feel is short-sighted and wrong. These are the ones where managing your contributions are key and will be the difference between being able to go back to your team pleased with the outcome, and going back to your team to begin a conversation that starts, "Well, you had better sit down…".

***a. Listen*** – We don't all think the same and therefore it is vital that you listen before you speak. Make sure you understand what other people are saying and try and see why they are saying it. What are their motivations? Can you change your contribution so that it meets more people's priorities?

***b. Stay patient, calm and sensible*** – It's easy when you feel strongly about something to get flustered and emotional, particularly when the values and principles at the root of our profession are being challenged or ignored. Make notes for what you want to say so that you give the facts, give a compelling argument and stay respectful and solution focussed.

***c. Time your intervention*** – When you do want to say something in a difficult or controversial discussion, think about your timing. It probably isn't best to say your piece too early. On contentious subjects, people walk into the room with their view and all they are thinking about is how to get it out. They aren't really listening to what others are saying. Sometimes, if you leave your contribution until others have spoken, you will get more traction and you can pick up on what others have said to give what you say more weight.

***d. Know when to back off*** – Choose your battles wisely and don't assume that everyone thinks like you do, they probably don't. You will need to see the bigger picture and compromise at some point. So, know when a tactical retreat is better and give yourself some space for manoeuvre. "I am happy to take this away with everyone's views and have a further chat with Fred and we can come back with some solutions," might prevent the risk of the chair just seeing it as a battle and outranking you with a decision you disagree with. In fact, the phrase, 'I will take that away and come back to you…' is a useful one generally in senior meetings.

**e. Know yourself** – As I said in chapter one of this section, if you know yourself well, you will know why you react a certain way in meetings and you will know how and when to intervene. Remember, you are different. Comms people are often the only people round the table who see things primarily from the people perspective. It is very easy to assume that everyone sees things like you do. They don't.

At a team awayday with my fellow directors they were told by the team dynamics expert to take particular note of what I said (hurray!) because I was the only person on the team who would bring that perspective. Without anyone else who would say what I was thinking, or perhaps anyone else who would agree with me, decisions could be skewed by the majority and therefore miss a crucial 'people' element to them.

A very typical discussion that demonstrates this is when to announce a redundancy or restructuring programme. The practical, plan-minded theorists might have worked out that the 22 December is when the letters should go out so that the three-month consultation period is concluded before the end of the financial year. The finance director wants the letters out as soon as possible because the money is draining fast; the chief executive just wants to get on with it; the operations director has several tricky staff issues that she wants sorted so also wants to get on with it. It is entirely possible that the comms director is the only person who says, "that's two days before Christmas. It will ruin people's holidays; morale will plummet and we could get slated on Twitter." Now, there are various views in the HR profession on whether it is better or worse to give people the Christmas period to think about their future, but the point I am making is that you might be the only person who sees the issue from the human perspective and raises it for discussion.

I guarantee that there will be senior team meetings where a plan will be presented by a fellow director, and you will think, "nobody is going to put up with that daft way of doing it - surely in a moment they are going to realise that the staff will just laugh." It seems so blatantly obvious to you. It is very possible that you are the only person who sees it that way, so be brave and say something.

**f. *Experience*** – Try and get some experience or training before you attend the first senior meeting in your new role. When I was a PR Manager at regional level in the NHS, I wasn't at all good at managing my interventions. I suffered from "say what you think loudly, early, and often" syndrome. In hindsight, it didn't work very well and left me frustrated. I phrase I had to learn, and to later teach others in my team was 'it's not sufficient just to be right.' Fortunately, I had a good boss who knew I would benefit hugely from training in managing and facilitating meetings and I did an impressive programme with the Civil Service College which included learning sets. This changed my practice markedly.

If you can't get training, then watch good people in the meetings that you do attend. Notice when and how they make their interventions, how they put an opposing view, how they try to reach a conclusion. And watch carefully, because the skills of the best people are quite subtle – the people who are loud and assertive might win on the day but probably won't be carrying people with them.

### Conclusion
In practical terms, managing up and across requires the same tips that you can read in any management textbook. The specifics of comms management are, I think, to understand

that you probably see things differently from others on the senior team so you can't speak in the same shorthand that you may do with your comms colleagues. And you may find that you are more affected by working relationships that are not harmonious than others. A general theme of this section is 'know yourself' and this is the best advice for these two situations.

Chapter Ten

# Managing your Team

- **Are comms people really all creative extroverts?**
- **What are the drivers for performance in comms teams?**
- **How do you empower the team when intuition is difficult to teach?**

I have done a fair bit of interim management in my later career. One of the joys is that I have worked with such a variety of good people, one of the strains is that, in a lot of cases, they wouldn't be bringing in an interim director if everything was going well so there are lots of management challenges.

There are plenty of books and courses on managing people. Here I have tried to pick out how some of these truths apply for communications directors.

You may have a wonderful team who love creativity, spontaneity, fun and ideas and hate process, theory and deadlines. You may be reporting to a chief executive who got where he is because he highly value goals, process, strategy and delivery. And you are stuck in between. How do you create the right environment for your team to be their best, while giving the boss confidence that they are delivering?

Everyone is different but, looking at comms teams generally, they are likely to be people who are 'people people'. They will have insight into how people tick, and they will prioritise relationships, understanding and harmony. They will be empathetic, kind, warm and compassionate.

They will also be creative people, liking ideas, often strategic and usually communicating well themselves (though this isn't always true). They are usually energetic, enthusiastic, loyal, supportive and good to work with.

You will have people, perhaps more on the campaigning or marketing side, who are very organised and efficient, practical and realistic in the way they approach their work. They will be energetic 'can-do' people who love finding solutions to challenges and diving in. They can be a bit impatient if asked to take a more thoughtful approach.

Comms people are often driven by their values. They want meaning from work and not just a day job to pay the mortgage. If their values are challenged, they feel it very deeply and may react strongly. These values might include honesty, inclusion and fairness. If anyone – particularly a senior person from another department – suggests something that doesn't meet these values, you may find yourself in fire-fighting mode.

You may also find that your team don't particularly like structure and process. There will be those, like yourself perhaps, who are on a management path so have either adapted to it or do work well with structure and process. And there will be those who are happy where they are, don't want to lead and feel really constrained and daunted by process, structure, theory and strategy. This can be frustrating for you or other colleagues. You may also find that the flip side of the more visionary skills of comms people is that they don't like detail. If you find you have someone in your team who is good with detail, they are a very valuable asset – keep them! You will probably need to build in processes that deal with this avoidance of detail.

For example, nobody can publish copy without a colleague checking it first for typos (the 'second eye').

It is also true that, if we aren't careful, comms people make their work-based decisions without enough reference to external factors such as data and evidence. We are often very intuitive, and this combined with our preference for prioritising people issues can mean that decisions are not as rounded as they might be. You will need to watch this. One of your team saying to you that they are 'absolutely sure' that option four is the way forward might be very true and honest for them, because that's what they feel, however you might have to ask a few questions to make sure that everything has been properly considered.

You may also find that your team are more sensitive to criticism, sometimes seeing criticism when it isn't really there. They will need a lot of praise, encouragement and credit for their successes to keep them motivated.

You will also need to be mindful that within a team that largely displays these characteristics you will have people who don't. Your photographer who doesn't really like working with people and doesn't communicate very well, your business manager who takes no prisoners when it comes to getting the processes and paperwork right. It's easy for these individuals to feel isolated because everyone assumes that comms teams are all gregarious wordsmiths.

## 1. Letting go, keeping a grip

You got to the top because you are pretty good at your job. Your practical skills are vital to the organisation. So, it's very important that you continue to write all the news releases, proofread every publication, oversee the design of every page of the website, do all the one-to-one conversations with journalists, chair all the customer reference groups and attend every planning meeting for the annual conference. Plus, of course, attending the weekly senior managers team meeting, the Board meeting, the strategic review meeting, the weekly operational meeting etc etc. There are enough hours in the day if you use those ones that happen when everyone else is asleep. Let's not waste, them, eh?

Or perhaps not. News sense, negotiation skills, topical comment in 140 characters. You may better at these things than your team. But when you are in charge you have to let go a bit and let your team do the day-to-day work.

Stepping up the ladder requires taking your feet off the rungs below. It's difficult because your skills include a level of judgement and experience that, perhaps, your team don't have. Yes, you probably can write a better press release, and perhaps it does annoy you that you have to keep suggesting a different top line, but that is what the job is. Enabling, training, empowering your team to do the job but otherwise getting out of the way so that you can do the new job.

If you always work more hours than there are in the day you are possibly cheating not learning. Deciding what not to do, what to delegate, what to let go without you even seeing it – these are key judgements.

The reputation of the organisation is a finely balanced thing. You need to make sure that you have enough grip to ensure that bad mistakes aren't made, and the senior team have confidence in you. At the same time, you need to let go sufficiently to allow your team to flourish and to see you modelling good working practice.

Make sure your own senior team know what you want to check and what you don't. I found that a weekly note at the end of the week from them of what was happening was useful, and a Monday 'heads-up' meeting so you can discuss the week and get more involved if you want to. You also do a note, and in the weekly meeting you say what you are doing, too. Part of your job is ensuring that you empower your team by helping them know the full context. You also never know if they will need to answer a question from the chief executive if you aren't around.

One of the common issues with a comms team is that you will have staff who deal directly with the chief executive without your involvement. This is often true of the chief press officer and the internal comms manager. You may not be involved in all these discussions, but you need to ensure that they know that they can and must tell you about any issues and that they have access to your expertise. This is partly because you will have useful experience and knowledge to apply but also because you must protect your team from bearing a weight of responsibility that is above their level. If something goes wrong, it is not right or fair that they should be blamed and take the rap for it. Equally, if you breathe down their necks all the time, they won't take responsibility at all and you will probably hold up the process.

In the first part of the book we talked about strategy and planning. This is where you set the direction that helps your team to control the scale of their jobs. What can they say 'no' to? What is a priority? Of the 100 things that they could be doing, which ten are going to get done that day? As mentioned before, you will have people in your team who hate strategy and planning, but when it converts into whether they have too much work to do, and too much pressure on them, they will be more interested. It's your role to give them the boundaries and tools to make the job doable.

## 2. Managing your direct reports

In an interim director role, I came out of my first full directors' meeting and immediately asked my team heads to sit down with me so I could debrief. There were wide eyes and shocked looks around the table. Their previous director hadn't done that – they didn't know at first whether I was dumping on them or empowering them.

It's obvious to say, but your job will be so much easier if your direct reports do their jobs well. And a lot of this is down to you. A temptation is to assume that your direct reports are not going to be interested in all the boring governance and board-level strategy meetings that you sit in. Partly true, partly not. They probably need and want to know more than you think.

The risk with having good people is that you take them for granted. Make sure that they get the time and support from you that they need to do their jobs to the very best of their ability.

"What happened at Exec Meeting?" asks your head of media. "Nothing much, usual boring stuff," you joke. What does this say to them? "Don't worry yourselves about that stuff"? "I can't trust you with this information"? It took me a while to realise the importance of giving the senior team more information on what was being discussed at Board and Exec meetings (though obviously not the highly confidential information – that's not fair on them.) Most people do their jobs better if they know the wider context, but particularly comms people.

The quick debrief after each exec meeting has the advantage for me of getting to them before any of the other directors with any follow up actions and my own thoughts on them. ("I said you would help Ann with the publicity for the 14th but in my view she is overselling it. You might want to give it a light touch.") It also means I can give them some of the wider context of what is going on for other directorates. Comms people are curious by nature. They may as well get the news from you (even if you think it's irrelevant) rather than get a version from elsewhere. It's difficult to carve out the time for these chats with your senior team but it pays for itself hugely and builds trust.

Don't forget, too, that you are responsible for building a team that can be stable when you are away, or if you leave. Are you investing time in enabling them to be the stand-in director? Part of the job here is ensuring that they each respect each others' disciplines. If they have to stand in for you at the exec meeting, or for your two-week holiday, they will need to know what's happening across all the teams in your remit.

### How to manage people whose job you can't do
The operations director pointed at me across the board-room table. "You will know Jude. As I understand it, the Local Authority Social Services Complaints Regulations have a criterion for determining who can make a complaint. But how do we interpret that provision and is this complainant eligible?"

"Erm…good question Paul. I would have to check that and get back to you…"

For the first time, I had people reporting to me whose jobs I couldn't do. In fact, not just couldn't do, but I couldn't even busk an answer.

As director of comms this might be the first time you manage disciplines other than your own profession. For me, the rigorously controlled and statutory rules for social care complaints was one. I had an excellent team, thankfully, but I had to represent this subject at the Boardroom table.

This isn't a situation exclusive to comms people of course, but comms is one profession where you can get all the way to Director just doing what you are good at.   This isn't true for every profession.  At director level though you might find that you are responsible for several different teams.  In my own experience this has included policy, advocacy, customer service, marketing, complaints, equality and diversity and the library.   Other roles often have corporate affairs or strategy included.  And in the comms role you may have senior staff who are more experienced than you at social media, or engagement, or events-management.

If you are in this situation, recognise that you are benefitting from a new set of skills and experience in your top team and this can be really valuable.  Project management, data management, research – these talents can really strengthen your team.

At first you may not be able to comment on the specifics of the operation, but once you have taken the time to understand it better, you can ensure that it fits into the broader strategy and it will be your role to advise on how the main issues are played through the executive team and Board. This means advising on how papers and discussions are handled.  It is partly about creating the space for your team to do their jobs properly.  You will also need to hold your team accountable for meeting their objectives.

In the research chapter I mentioned that when I first worked in commercial PR, we were still in the days of measuring press cuttings for judging results. The managing director, a salesman by background, didn't really know how to set objectives for the PR officer.  He asked me how many column inches of press cuttings I thought I could generate in a month, he then added 25 per cent and told me that was my target.  He didn't really understand my world, but he managed to create a team atmosphere for all of us that meant we wanted to do well, we wanted to work hard.  I could have fiddled my results – he was never going to measure,  but I didn't want to.

### 3. Encouraging the team

The results of the 360-degree appraisal were in front of me. Like most people I skimmed over the positive stuff and lingered on the negatives. "Needs to be more visible".

If your team gets bigger than the immediate area where you work, visibility is a real issue.  Depending on how extraverted you are, walking the floor and chatting to people is either easy or something to be dreaded.  But people do appreciate it. My secret weapon is my Chelsea FC mug.  I am a keen football supporter and I find that if I carry my cup of tea around the office, and onto the other floors, I get lots of banter about my team that makes it easier to chat to people and then ask them how the job is going.

Remembering the personality types of comms people, you will know that they will need a lot of praise, encouragement and credit.

I had an interim job where I saw a supervisor regularly taking credit for his team's work.  I saw the life-juice being sucked out of them as he always talked about their items on the team meeting agenda, rewrote their emails so that they looked like updates to senior managers from him and generally did far too much telling off and too little praise. This was a very busy, stressful project and the team needed his encouragement not his criticism.

There is definitely a place for the firm hand – you will have people in the team for whom targets, objectives and deadlines just aren't their priority – but encouragement is the fuel that will largely work with these types of people, particularly in a team environment. Comms personality types largely aren't the people who are looking to climb on their colleagues to reach the top, they are co-operative, harmony-orientated people. This means they could be very demotivated if they perceive you are treating one of the team unfairly.

## 4. Targets

A particular challenge for comms directors is setting meaningful targets. This is discussed more fully in the research and evaluation chapter  but within the context of managing the team remember that they are looking to you for direction, and the targets and strategy are an important tool for this.  And this is a role that you can't delegate (although you will take advice from your direct reports). You have to take the tough decisions on which work and projects will not be done, as much as about which projects will. This isn't easy, but you are doing your team a disservice if you don't shoulder this responsibility and get it approved through the chief executive if necessary.

This will also be modelling a strategic approach to your own team. It is my view that this is an under-recognised skill among comms people who are able to get a long way in the profession without necessarily having training or experience in strategy-setting even though they do often have the ability to think strategically.  It is crucial that they see their director of comms thinking, acting and questioning in a strategic manner. What are we really trying to achieve? Is it realistic? Who are the priority audiences? Do we really know what they think?

## 5. Creativity

I had attended an excellent course on encouraging creativity, and I wanted to try some of my new learning on the team. Lesson one, we can't just be creative, we must warm up the creative parts of our brain. So, we had assembled for the usual team meeting, with its usual agenda, boring meeting room and familiar crazy time constraints. "Before we start," I said hesitantly, "I would like us all to think of as many uses as we can for a paperclip." It felt to me like the request jarred with the normal atmosphere for these meetings, but the team went with it. They got into some great conversations and there was a bit of laughter. I felt that loosening up a bit enhanced our discussion as we got to the items on the agenda that needed a bit of creative thought, but I can't be certain. But I couldn't start every meeting with that type of question, could I?

I have worked in lots of comms teams. I have never seen an in-house comms team that has cracked this issue about encouraging creativity – despite the fact that creativity is our bread-and-butter.

How many boring meetings have we sat in where the chair asks, "has anyone got any bright ideas on how we can launch this initiative?" We then feel that our brains are stuck in a treacly darkness as we try and dredge up an original thought. And yet, put us in the pub later having a laugh with everyone chipping in and suddenly we have lots of ideas.

In contrast, I have seen agencies who thoroughly recognise the need to find ways to release the creative energy and ideas of their team. I remember being shown round the new offices of one such agency. It was the third set of offices that they had been in and they had learned from each former place how important it was to create a physical space that encouraged creativity. It had comfy sofas, lots of inspiring books, lots of light, some games.

We tried to create such a space in one place I worked. The head of the creative team – which numbered about 20 people – asked me if we could refurbish a little-used space and give it some good AV equipment, some display spaces and a funkier feel. It took some persuasion to get it past the estates team, but we did it. It was a small step, but it did make a difference.

I don't have all the answers on this, so my one piece of advice is to recognise this as an issue and don't automatically expect that you or your team will be at their creative best within the confines – culturally and physically – of the normal, stressed office environment.

## Conclusion

Managing your team can be such an exciting job. You are likely to have people who are passionate, thoughtful, sensitive, creative and hard-working. They will give you the 'legs' to do so much more than you could do by yourself – especially if you give them the encouragement, guidance and space. At the same time each of these positives has a flip side that you need to be aware of so that you can ensure the team performs at its best, and – importantly for your senior colleagues – appears to perform at its best. Comms teams can be a breath of fresh air in an office environment and, with the right support, also make a huge difference to meeting the company goals.

## Chapter Eleven
# Your Communications Career

- **Are you too grand for professional training?**
- **How do you break out of your comfort zone?**
- **Is it time for a management qualification?**

Perhaps you are on the communications career ladder, looking to get to director of comms. Here are some thoughts on how to get ahead.

### Professional training

Should you get professional training? I did a comms degree and my post-graduate diploma in public relations, so I probably come at this question with a biased view. The degree was useful but not essential and I would have appreciated it more if I had done it later. The post-graduate qualification was invaluable, particularly because I did it in when I was already doing the job so I could apply what I was learning.

The professional qualification is a fast track to understanding the breadth of the job and suggested processes and strategies to deal with different things. Of course, you can do the job without it, and very good people do. However, you are then very reliant on working for good people who will model and teach the job properly.

I remember moving to a new job as PR Manager in the public sector. I had done one previous PR job for a national firm of estate agents where I only did two things: trying to get media coverage and putting together the staff magazine. My first job in the public sector opened my eyes to planning, strategy and making sure that different stakeholders were engaged and informed. Having come from journalism originally, I honestly thought that PR people mostly just sent out press releases. I absolutely loved finding out what the job really was. I was very lucky to be working for such good people from whom I learned a huge amount. Not every new comms person has this luxury and I am very grateful.

I would especially recommend training if you find that your job is very focussed just on one area of the role such as media, or events. Learning how to set what you do into a broader context, and to understand strategies, will be very valuable to you.

## Media relations, social media and digital

You can't escape the fact that media and social media relations are nearly always the core of what we do and are regarded by some people (including our bosses) as all that we do. There is a well-trodden route into the profession from journalism. I would recommend everyone who wants to get on in comms to get media experience early if they can – either by working as a journalist or by working in a busy press office where there is lots of reactive work. And I would recommend anyone who comes into comms from journalism to do professional training, particularly to learn about strategy, otherwise you will gravitate towards getting over-involved in the media work because it's what you know.

Similarly, if you only ever done media relations and/or social media then it is good to get a job with wider experience fairly early on if you want to climb the ladder.

## Ongoing training and development

Unfortunately, most people in comms don't follow a set path of training and development. You can get to senior roles in the profession with only a limited view of the job, which is a real shame. I would recommend everyone to get training in strategic planning which I have observed is a weakness and isn't always modelled well, and then training in areas of the job that you are less familiar with such as social media or internal comms.

As you climb the management ladder, of course, you will need to work on management skills, and you may choose to do an MBA.

For your own development it helps to work for good people. This is probably true of most jobs, but it's certainly true in comms where you can learn a lot from the judgement and instinct of a skilled person. I have been fortunate enough to have worked for some of the best and I hope that I have reflected some of this learning in this book.

## Conclusion

Comms is a great career, often at the very heart of an organisation's success or failure. But, in my opinion, it is a profession with a set of specific skills that can't just be mastered by someone who is very active on Facebook, or who writes well. Invest in training and diversify your experience to be at your most effective.

And while learning all of this, don't forget the basic human values of how to treat people well. In 1936 Dale Carnegie wrote *How to Win Friends and Influence People*. It became a worldwide bestseller and is still worth a read now. In his introduction he quotes John D Rockefeller who said, "the ability to deal with people is as purchasable a commodity as sugar or coffee. And I will pay more for that ability than for any other under the sun." That's the heart of our role and it has never been more important.

Good luck!

# Acknowledgements

I have been fortunate to work with many great people in my career, both communications professionals and fellow directors. So, most of the learning in this book is my own version of what I have learnt from you all. Thank you.

I would also like to thank the various teams that I have been privileged to manage. Every good example in this book happened because skilled professionals were doing their jobs very well. Thanks for all you achieved, and apologies for not always practising what I preach.

Thanks also to James Humphreys for suggesting that I write this book, and for his help in getting it right; Robin Banerji and Helen McCallum for reading the drafts and improving them considerably; my friends for putting up with me saying "I am writing a book" at every opportunity and my wonderful husband Ali for patiently hearing that phrase more often than anyone else.

*More from IndieBooks...*

# WILLIAMS ON PUBLIC DIPLOMACY

A practitioner's guide to one of the most influential and least-known arts of communication. John Williams' career at the highest levels of journalism and public service has seen him at the side of successive UK Foreign Secretaries, helping to shape the way Britain is seen around the world. In this book he explains how governments try to shape public opinion in other countries, what they hope to gain, and what it means for peace, prosperity and human rights. Using real-world examples from Indi-Pakistan to Israel-Palestine, and giving advice on best practice and pitfalls, Williams gives a unique, working-level insight into this powerful diplomatic tool.

*John Williams was Political Editor of the Daily Mirror before becoming press secretary to FOreign Secretary Robin Cook. He was also Head of News at the UK Foreign and Commonwealth Office to Cook's successors, Jack Straw and Margaret Beckett. He now advises governments and other clients internationally on communications and public diplomacy.*

# SERVE TO LEAD

## The British Army Anthology on Leadership

The original British Army anthology on leadership, used to train generations of officers, brings together the collected wisdom of great military leaders, tacticians and historians with the authentic voices of unknown soldiers. Moving, inspiring, amusing and thought-provoking, it teaches lessons about motivation, leadership and morale that are every bit as valuable to today's leaders and managers. Complete with a new introduction by Robin Matthews, who commanded the Light Dragoons in Iraq, on the background to Serve to Lead and its relevance to his own career and experiences from Sierra Leone to Afghanistan.